HORROR
IN THE EAST

HORROR
IN THE EAST

Laurence Rees

BBC

To Benedict Rees and Ann Cattini

PICTURE CREDITS

Plate Section 1
Mainichi, Tokyo; Mainichi; NARA; Popperfoto; Hulton Getty; NARA; Hulton Getty; Hulton Getty;
Hulton Getty; Hulton Getty; Mainichi; Imperial War Museum.
Plate Section 2
Hulton Getty; Hulton Getty; Jan Ruff; Masayo Enomoto; Popperfoto; Imperial War Museum;
Naruto House; Imperial War Museum; Hulton Getty; Australian War Memorial;
Australian War Memorial; Bill Hedges; Hulton Getty; NARA.
Plate Section 3
Kenichiro Oonuki; Hulton Getty; Hulton Getty; NARA; Ralph Crane/Timepix; Hulton Getty;
Yoshiko Hashimoto; Ishikawa Kiyoko; Ishikawa Kiyoko; NARA; Hulton Getty; NARA;
Michael Witowich; Hulton Getty; Corbis.

Published to accompany the television series *Horror in the East*, first broadcast on BBC2 in 2000.
Writer and producer: Laurence Rees

Published by BBC Worldwide Ltd, Woodlands, 80 Wood Lane, London W12 0TT

First published in 2001 © Laurence Rees 2001
The moral right of the author has been asserted.

ISBN 0 563 53426 5

Commissioning editor: Sally Potter
Project editor: Sarah Lavelle Copy editor: Esther Jagger
Art director: Linda Blakemore Designer: Ann Thompson
Picture researchers: Tanya Batchelor and Miriam Hyman
Cartographer: Olive Pearson

Set in Perpetua
Printed in Great Britain by Butler and Tanner Ltd, Frome
Jacket and plate sections printed by Lawrence-Allen Ltd, Weston-super-Mare

CONTENTS

FOREWORD

Can history be shared? This is the key question Laurence Rees raises in this important book. And the book gives a resoundingly affirmative response to that question.

There is a temptation to view a nation's past primarily, if not entirely, in the national framework: to consider its history as *sui generis*, a product of its own culture, to be understood in the context of its own indigenous development. A recent school textbook in Japan – one that has aroused a storm of protest from Korea, China, and other countries – states that there are as many histories as there are nations, with the implication that a country's history must be comprehended, appreciated, and judged in terms of its people's ideas, interests, and values. Defenders of this sort of self-centred nationalism – and such people are found everywhere – believe that a given people 'understand' their history better than other peoples, and that foreigners should not stand in judgment over it.

Horror in the East, both as a documentary and as a book, takes the opposite view. It has been produced on the assumption that the past must be shared, that it is open to anyone to examine, and that the quest for historical understanding knows no national boundaries. Japanese, Chinese, Koreans, Filipinos, Australians, Americans, British, and others who appear in the book (and in the documentary film) all seek to understand, whether as participants in past dramas or as contemporary commentators, the human tragedy that was the horror in Asia during the Second World War.

To speak of 'horror', of course, implies moral judgment. But the judgment is not necessarily that of one nation condemning another nation, for no nation is free of moral culpability. Rather, the judgment is, first, the application of universal human standards to specific deeds of

barbarism committed by individuals; it is, second, an effort to understand why atrocities of such magnitude were perpetrated at specific
moments in time; it is, finally, an act of linking the present to the past in
which today's generation speaks to an earlier generation.

The book is rich in detail, containing some episodes the BBC team
discovered in dust-covered archives in Japan, the United States, Britain,
the Netherlands, Australia and elsewhere. The interviews, especially of
Japanese veterans, are vivid reminders of what it was like to live, and to
face certain death, in 'the valley of darkness', the term that is often used
to describe the war years. There are no taboos in the story; Rees, for
instance, asks pertinent questions about the role of the emperor and
examines them dispassionately, avoiding dogmas and emotional rhetoric.
Above all, the book succeeds in putting Japan's wartime policies and
behaviour in the context of a conformist society under pressure. As one
who grew up during the war – I was in fifth grade when the war ended
– I can attest to the truth of this argument. The power of conformism,
the ardent wish not to be different, a misguided sense of honour which
dictates that dissent will disgrace the nation, the family, and yourself –
these traits still exist in Japan, and in many other countries, today. But
the book suggests that there are others, those who are willing to speak
candidly about the past, not merely among themselves but also with
people from other lands. To the extent that *Horror in the East* reveals the
existence of such people, the book points to the emergence of an international arena where memory and history may be shared and openly discussed, where what the author aptly refers to as 'a common thread'
transcending national or cultural differences may be found.

Professor Akira Iriye
Harvard University

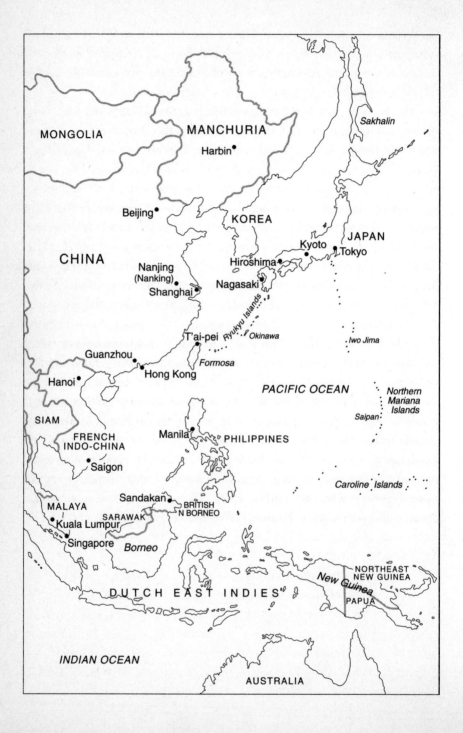

INTRODUCTION

'Inscrutable' – that is the adjective most often used to describe the Japanese. And on the face of it, what could be more 'inscrutable' than their actions during the Second World War? Their attack on Pearl Harbor, their worship of their emperor as a God, their willingness to die in kamikaze attacks, their appalling treatment of Allied prisoners of war, their war crimes against women and children in China – all these actions and more are hard, if not impossible, for Westerners to understand.

I fully expected to run into this concrete wall of 'inscrutability' in our quest to understand why the Japanese acted as they did during the war – just as I had when, years before, I had asked an intelligent, sophisticated Japanese friend what she knew about the most infamous atrocity committed by the Imperial Army, the Nanking massacre of 1937. 'Ah,' she replied, smiling, 'I did study history at school, but you must understand, Japanese history is many thousands of years old and very complex. It's a very, very big book we have to study. And, of course, we start at the beginning of the history and study hard and in detail. So, unfortunately, by the time I left school we hadn't finished the whole history.... I think perhaps we stopped at the end of the nineteenth century. We just didn't get around to looking at the Nanking massacre.'

The desire of many Japanese to answer uncomfortable questions in a similarly evasive way, and so preserve the harmony of their society, is intense. No one spends more than a few weeks in Japan without discovering the Japanese desire to 'fit in' to their society, to preserve the *wa* as they put it, the solidarity of the group, by reaching consensus and by obeying the rules. Most Japanese are concerned, to a degree unheard of in the West, about how others perceive them; there is even a word for the phobia, *taikinkyofusho* – the fear of what other people think of them.

But unlike the majority of Japanese our interviewees did decide to act against the *wa*, the consensus of the group, and I am profoundly grateful to them for that decision. For if this book has a value, it lies in the first-hand testimonies of those whom we questioned. Academic historians rarely have the inclination or the training to trace war criminals and cross-question them about their actions, so this is an area in which the techniques of journalism can help historical understanding. Whilst the period covered by this book (from the Japanese aggression in China in the 1930s through to the dropping of the atomic bombs in August 1945) is so long that, inevitably, not all of the detailed history could be covered, the testimony we gathered does, I believe, offer a valuable insight into the mentality of those who took part in this terrible war – an insight that scholarly works sometimes lack.

I was astonished at the depth of the material we did eventually obtain from our Japanese interviewees. From the son who murdered his mother in a suicide pact to the self-confessed rapist; from the doctor who performed medical experiments on Chinese prisoners to the guard who shot Allied prisoners on a death march, our interviewees were for the most part open and frank. Perhaps the most revelatory interview is that with a kamikaze pilot – cheated of death by the mechanical failure of his aircraft – who explains convincingly why he simultaneously believed that the suicide mission he was asked to embark on was a crazy idea, and yet still felt compelled to volunteer for it. The straightforward – often self-incriminating – manner in which these veterans answered our questions was in many ways extraordinary, given the cultural imperative in Japan that dissuades many from speaking openly and critically about the war.

Our Japanese interviewees chose to talk to us for a variety of reasons; some were clearly persuaded because they trusted the BBC not to misuse their words, others because they had a genuine desire to try to make foreigners understand why they had acted as they did. Still more – having already been imprisoned by the Chinese for their crimes – felt free to incriminate themselves with impunity. But the overwhelming reason why many were willing to be questioned so provocatively about their actions was because they are coming to the end of their lives and want to put on record, warts and all, their part in what happened.

This inquiry into the mind-set of those who took part in the Pacific War is the last in a trilogy of projects I have written and produced on the Second World War, and in the Postscript at the end of this book I explore some of the ways in which meeting so many veterans from different nationalities has altered my thinking about the conflict. It is sufficient here to record that, after listening to many of our Japanese interviewees, I came to realize that they were not so very different from the German and Russian veterans I had met before.

It turns out that the Japanese are not 'inscrutable' after all. A combination of cultural belief and geographical and historical circumstance caused Japanese society to evolve, in the first half of the twentieth century, to a point where the very human desire to belong, to fit in, to be part of the group had been elevated to an all-embracing quasi-religion. It needed only a group of ardent militaristic nationalists to make of this society a powerful and fanatical weapon, able to produce an army capable of great crimes.

The truth is that we should be concerned about what the Japanese did during the Second World War and the years that immediately preceded it not because they are somehow utterly 'alien', but because their history tells us how dangerous it is to be human and to long, at all costs, to conform.

Laurence Rees
London
April 2001

THE CHINA SOLUTION

According to popular myth the infamous behaviour of the Japanese during the Second World War has one basic cause: the Japanese were a uniquely cruel people, brainwashed after centuries of adherence to a warrior code that celebrated atrocity and encouraged torture, and conditioned by universal emperor worship. The surprise, so this comfortable theory goes, is not that so many prisoners of war were mistreated, but that the toll of misery was not even higher. In short, the Japanese were (and perhaps still are) an inhuman people from an inhuman culture. The great advantage of this prevalent myth is that it renders any real study of the history of Japan in the twentieth century unnecessary. But this theory does have one disadvantage – it is demonstrably wrong.

During the First World War the Japanese fought on the same side as the British and captured some 4600 prisoners of war in the German colony of Tsintao on the Asian mainland. If the popular myth is correct, these European soldiers ought to have become victims of the inherent Japanese cruelty. But they were not. Far from it. 'They were treated as guests at that time,' says Hans Kettle, whose grandfather was one of the German prisoners of war in Japan. 'They had a lot of free time in the camp. They made their own sausages, they had a gymnastic club, they did a lot of musicals.' Herr Kettle summed up his grandfather's experience of imprisonment at the hands of the Japanese in one simple phrase – 'I think he had a nice time.' Far from forming the view as a result of his years as a prisoner of war that the Japanese were a cruel people, his grandfather stayed on in Japan after his release and married a young Japanese woman. His grandson still lives there and runs a successful German restaurant in Tokyo.

The experience of Hans Kettle's grandfather is not unique. Virtually all of these Germans were well treated by their Japanese captors. The death rate amongst the Germans was extremely low – 1.2 per cent. And a wonderful collection of photographs of the German POWs in Bando camp survives, showing them fit, healthy and thriving – frolicking in the water and then drinking beer in their comfortable camp. Their experience was more like a healthy weekend scouting exercise than the horrors of *The Bridge on the River Kwai*. Such Japanese kindness was not just confined to treatment of prisoners in the First World War. In 1905, during the Russo–Japanese War, F.A. Mackenzie, special correspondent of the *Daily Mail*, wrote, 'It is impossible to speak too highly of the great care and attention which the Japanese people show their stricken enemies.'

All of which leaves a history which is at once more intriguing and complex than the popular myth of the Japanese as universally cruel, and also begs the crucial question, when and how did this Japanese attitude of generosity in war change?

These European prisoners of war were benefiting from an imperial command of 1880 that called on the Japanese armed forces to treat captured prisoners with respect. This imperial command, in turn, was influenced by the prevailing Japanese desire to act like a modern, Western nation and by a wish to emphasize the elements of compassion that had always existed in the Japanese warrior code.

It is common knowledge that Japan had been a country effectively isolated from the rest of the world until the second half of the nineteenth century. Equally well known is Japan's headlong desire in the years that followed to adopt Western inventions and industry. But far less well known is the political revolution that was occurring at the same time – a revolution that would have far-reaching consequences. Central to this revolution was the seismic change in the role of the emperor. There had been an emperor on the throne of Japan for two thousand years – but for the last six hundred, under the dominance of the Shogun (the most powerful warlord in the country) and the warrior elite, the emperor had held little real power, considered too 'special' to be bothered with real governance. It had been successive Shoguns who had dominated Japan.

The arrival of Commander Matthew Perry and his American warships in Tokyo Bay in 1853 on their mission to open Japan to international trade was the catalyst not just for the Japanese desire to learn Western technology, but also for profound political change. In the argument and confusion that swept through the Japanese elite in the wake of Perry's visit, power began to seep slowly back to the emperor as infighting grew between the rival clans that together had dominated the Shogunate. In the midst of this conflict, Emperor Komei died in February 1867 and was succeeded by Meiji, his fifteen-year-old son. It was to be a new beginning for the institution of the emperor.

After Emperor Meiji's succession the Japanese did not just try to learn the industrial secrets of the West (whilst cleverly ensuring that their industrial base remained under Japanese ownership); they also began to examine the political processes of the foreigners – in particular studying the democratic systems of Britain and the USA. During the 1880s Emperor Meiji and his advisers discussed what political shape the new Japan should have. One of those whom they consulted was the former US President, Ulysses S. Grant. Ironically, given that the political solution which resulted was to help cause many of the subsequent problems that the USA encountered with Japan, Grant cautioned against allowing any new parliament too much power.[1] Eventually, in February 1889, the Meiji constitution was unveiled. The first elected parliament of Japan was created – the Imperial Diet. But only property owners (less than 2 per cent of the population) were enfranchized. The over-arching concern of the framers of the constitution was to consolidate the new powers of the emperor. From the first, this was no British style constitutional monarchy. No criticism of the emperor was to be permitted. Only the emperor could declare war and only the emperor could make peace. And since the emperor was, under the constitution, supreme commander of the armed forces, the heads of the army and navy swiftly claimed the right to report direct to him, bypassing the elected cabinet. (A further consequence of the new political system established by the Meiji constitution was to give even more power and control to the armed forces. The army and navy ministers who were members of the cabinet could only be appointed from the ranks of retired or serving generals or admirals. This meant that if they resigned and no suitable general or admiral was willing to replace them, the government would fall. It was as if the system had been designed to create a military that could not be controlled by the elected representatives of the people.)

As the nineteenth century came to a close the Japanese had adopted a new constitution, had introduced heavy industry to their country and were building a modern army. Now they looked at the powerful Western nations and learnt there was one more attribute they needed in order to be considered a powerful, sophisticated nation — colonies. Virtually all of Southeast Asia was under foreign domination — the British ruled Burma and Malaya, the Dutch the East Indies and the French today's Vietnam, Laos and Cambodia. The lesson the Japanese took from this was clear; strong nations had the right — almost the obligation — to dominate weaker ones. As soon as they felt powerful enough the Japanese moved on their neighbours Korea and Taiwan (then called Formosa). In the hope of halting Japanese aggression on the Asian mainland, in 1894 the Chinese signed a treaty that gave Taiwan to Japan — an act that demonstrated to the Japanese how weak the once mighty empire of China, now torn apart by internal conflict, had become. Similarly, the Russian Empire discovered the power of the imperial armed forces when, in 1904, Japanese ships sank the Tsar's fleet in a surprise attack at Port Arthur. Korea was also brought under Japanese control and formally made part of the Japanese 'Empire' in 1910. During the First World War the Japanese, obliged to fight on the British side as the result of another treaty, gained further colonies, this time at the expense of Germany — Kiaochao in China and the Mariana, Caroline and Marshall islands in the Pacific. Then, in 1915, with the West distracted by the war in Europe, the Japanese moved their army deeper into Manchuria, occupying key positions in order to 'protect their interests'. The First World War ended with Japan's position as the most modern, powerful, industrialized nation in Asia confirmed. It is hardly surprising, therefore, that during this period the Japanese treated European prisoners humanely — was Japan not effectively a European nation itself?

While their army triumphed over Japan's neighbours abroad, at home in 1925 the vote was given to every Japanese adult. On the surface, democracy seemed entrenched. Political parties argued with each other as Japanese women shopped for Western-style clothes and goods in the Ginza in Tokyo. In the early 1920s Crown Prince Hirohito went on a much-publicized visit to Britain and played golf with the Prince of Wales. It was as if all Japan had heeded the words of the popular slogan, first coined by an academic in 1885, 'Abandon Asia – go for the West!' But all this was only on the surface. The most significant legacy of the Meiji constitution remained etched into this new Japanese society – the most decidedly non-Western power of the monarch. And, most crucially of all, the emperor of Japan was, as a direct result of the Meiji restoration, now considered by his subjects to be more than a mere human being. A few Japanese had always acted as if their emperor was divine, but to the majority of Japanese pre-Meiji the emperor had been a remote figure, with no control over their lives. In the late nineteenth century all that had changed. In a conscious attempt by the monarchists to make the position of the emperor inviolable, Shinto (the ancient animistic religion of Japan) was made the state religion and it was decreed that the emperor, as a descendant of the sun-goddess, should be worshipped as a god. The importance of this conscious, political act cannot be over-estimated. The subsequent Japanese perception of their emperor was to condition virtually all their actions. 'The emperor at that time was called a "living god",' says Kenichiro Oonuki, a Japanese schoolboy during the 1920s. 'We were taught that the emperor was a god in the form of a human being. That was the education we received. When you think about it realistically, it is strange, and it's not possible, but that's what we were taught.' For Shigeaki Kinjou, growing up on the remote island of Tokashiki nearly 300 miles southeast of Tokyo, the pervasive belief that the emperor was a living god led to one simple conclusion: 'The Japanese people belonged to the emperor. We were his children.'

On Christmas Day 1926 the Emperor Meiji's grandson, a new 'living god', ascended the Japanese throne. He was a shy, bespectacled twenty-five-year-old, who would become known to the world as Emperor

Hirohito. His education had reflected the prevailing Japanese dichotomy. On the one hand he had received the traditional schooling, at the hands of senior military officers and other retainers, that befitted a future emperor; on the other he had developed a taste for modern science, particularly marine biology. He came to power in an era that had proved disastrous for monarchies around the world. Seven years earlier, as the First World War ended, the Kaiser had been forced from Germany, and only a few years before that the Tsar had been toppled in Russia. And now, throughout Europe in the aftermath of these revolutions, both intellectuals and labourers were becoming increasingly interested in the anti-religious, anti-monarchistic creed of communism.

In Japan, the years of strong leadership represented by the reign of the Emperor Meiji were far behind. The country had recently endured the rule of the Emperor Taisho, an ineffectual monarch who had been so incapable that Hirohito, his son, had acted as his regent since 1921. And in the wider world it appeared that the ruthless Darwinian ideals of the decades before the First World War, when all that mattered in the great land-grab race for colonies was who was stronger, were now out of fashion. Japanese delegates travelled to the Versailles and Washington conferences convened after the war and committed their country to a raft of treaties based on 'modern' principles aimed at the elimination of aggressive war and the peaceful solution of international problems through discussion and compromise in new institutions like the League of Nations.

Therefore as Hirohito came to the throne the paradox of his education and interests – half ancient tradition, half modern technology – was replicated in the country he ruled – half headlong search to embrace the values of the West, half the institutionalization of archaic beliefs. In such a situation the desire of the monarchists publicly to entrench the young emperor even more deeply in the minds of his subjects as a god is understandable. Now was not the time to show weakness and allow any discussion about the role of the monarchy, now was the time to embrace the values of the Meiji constitution – still less than forty years old – and confirm Hirohito as an ancient-style ruler of an ultra-modern society. This was the thinking behind the lengthy and elaborate series of ceremonies that marked Hirohito's accession to the throne, beginning with a glittering procession from the modern capital, Tokyo, to the traditional home of the emperor and sacred ancient capital, Kyoto, in November 1928. And it was no accident that only days after the elaborate religious (and often secret) ceremonies to confirm his divine right to rule, the young emperor attended a huge military review in Tokyo – the largest in the history of Japan. As 35,000 troops saluted him, it must have been clear to Hirohito which Japanese institution kept him securely in power. And, simultaneously, he must have taken comfort in the knowledge that the Meiji constitution allowed the commanders of the armed forces to report directly to him.

The immediate years after Hirohito's enthronement were unsettled in Japan. Just as in Germany, where the optimism of the Weimar Republic of the mid-1920s was crushed by the depression of the late 1920s and early 1930s, so in Japan the 'Western years' following the end of the First World War were not to endure. Many of the reasons for the subsequent unrest were shared by both countries. First, both Germany and Japan suffered sudden economic depression. Japan had already entered an agricultural slump before the Wall Street Crash of 1929 plunged the USA into financial catastrophe. With their own problems at home the Americans were now less keen on purchasing imported luxuries like silk, and many Japanese farmers went bankrupt. 'Here you couldn't find work – unemployment was high,' says Yoshio Tshuchiya who grew up in the north of Japan during the late 1920s. He remembers 'seven or eight' girls from his school being sold into prostitution by their parents. 'If they had money they didn't have to go,' he says. 'But because that family was poor, well, they went. I felt very sorry. Yes, I sympathized.'

Simultaneously with economic depression, Japan faced another problem that the Germans – especially the fledgling Nazi party – would have understood: the search for Lebensraum (living space). Many prominent Japanese felt there was simply not enough room in their country – the majority of which is mountainous and scarcely habitable – for the growing number of people. 'At the time the problem was our population was increasing,' says Masatake Okumiya, who held a senior position in the Imperial Navy during the Second World War, 'and our natural resources couldn't sustain the increase. Ideally we hoped to receive cooperation from other countries to solve the problem, but back then the world was under the control of the West and a peaceful solution seemed impossible.' Even more than in Germany, the perceived lack of living space dominated Japanese political discourse. The population density in Japan was one of the highest in the world. (Lack of space had for thousands of years conditioned Japanese culture. A society so crammed together is less likely to tolerate the disruptive individualist, and more emphasis has, out of geographical necessity, to be placed on the need for consensus and 'harmony' within the group.)

As Hirohito and the Japanese government wrestled with the problems of the depression and lack of living space, they acted to crush another threat that would have seemed familiar to the Nazi leadership – communism. In February 1928 left-wing parties in Japan gained eight seats in the national elections. Just over two weeks later the government sanctioned mass arrests of communists and Marxist sympathizers.

During the following year, there was more political instability when Hirohito demonstrated that he would be an aggressive player in the political arena by obtaining the resignation of prime minister Tanaka, a politician frequently criticized by the emperor. Here was further proof that Japan was demonstrably not a stable state ruled by a British-style constitutional monarch.

The extent of the growing fracture in the Japanese democratic process was emphasized still further when, in 1930, after Japan had signed the London Naval Treaty (which agreed comparative limits amongst the world's major navies), the new prime minister, Hamaguchi, was shot by an opponent of the agreement at Tokyo railway station. The message could not have been clearer – stand out against the growing nationalist spirit, personified by obsequious allegiance to the emperor and an increasing distrust of all things Western, only at great personal peril.

A growing faction within the Imperial Army wanted to dissociate Japan from the 'non-aggressive' values of the post-First World War treaties and return to the pursuit of the kind of colonial expansion that had so characterized Japanese behaviour in the late nineteenth and early twentieth centuries. The question these military figures (and many politicians on the right) posed was this: what had embracing the West's new-found love of peaceful compromise brought Japan in the 1920s? The answer seemed clear: economic depression, the unsolved problem of shortage of living space, and the 'infection' of Japanese society with dangerous Western values like the emancipation of women, universal suffrage and communism. Japan's difficulties, so the right-wing argument went, could only be solved by a combination of turning against the West and expansion through military action.

Throughout the summer of 1931 the belief had been growing within the Imperial Army that Japan's problems could best be alleviated by taking complete control of Manchuria, a land rich in everything Japan was not – chiefly space and natural resources – just 700 miles northwest of Tokyo across the Sea of Japan. General Jiro Minami, minister of war, made a speech in August that all but demanded the army should act of its own volition and attack. But senior officers like Minami knew that formal authorization for such an action was impossible – it would be against all the treaties Japan had recently signed. An excuse for Japanese aggression would have to be manufactured – and it duly was. On 18 September Japanese army units blew up a section of the Japanese-controlled South Manchurian Railway but claimed that the Chinese had done it. Acting on their own initiative units of the Japanese Kwantung army moved forward to engage nearby Chinese forces. Within days the invaders had captured Kirin, the local capital and made their ally, a local Chinese warlord, declare independence. By February 1932 the Japanese had conquered Manchuria and established a puppet state under Emperor Henry Pu-yi. He announced the establishment of the state of Manchukuo – new 'living space' for the Japanese.

The conquest of Manchuria was the crucial moment at which Japan's real estrangement from the Western democracies began. It was a source of conflict that was not resolved until the end of the Second World War. As Japanese troops moved to create the new puppet state, Hirohito faced a moment of decision – should he accept or reject the army's actions?

After due consideration he did what, throughout his rule, he would do so often at moments of crisis – nothing. From the moment he first heard of the unilateral action of the Kwantung army in Manchuria to the eventual subjugation of the Manchurian people, Hirohito took no effective steps to bring his troops to account. On the one hand he was the supreme commander of the Imperial Army and could have demanded the aggression be halted, on the other he was conscious that the chief reason he remained in power was the support of the armed forces. After all, it had not been so long ago that a powerful military figure, the Shogun, had sidelined the emperor into effective impotence. It was a moment in history that called for courage and leadership from a Japanese emperor bolstered by the powers granted him by the Meiji constitution. But Hirohito failed the test and in the process failed his nation's fledgling democracy.

Of course, there is another explanation besides weakness for Hirohito's inaction during this period. It is very possible that he approved of what his army was doing. It was clear they were winning the war in Manchuria, and Japanese newspapers were full of jingoistic sentiment – an emotional reaction that caught the mood of the majority of the Japanese. Manchuria was for the Japanese what California had been to the Americans ninety years before – a land of potential riches, full of exploitable natural resources. 'I wanted to go to Manchuria and earn money,' says Yoshio Tsuchiya who enlisted in the Imperial Army in 1931. 'I wanted to earn money and be able to build a house for my family. If I stayed on in Manchuria I thought I could send money back home.'

In October 1931 the political instability worsened when a group of army officers led by Colonel Hashimoto and Major Cho of the ultra-right-wing 'Cherry Blossom' society attempted to overthrow the civilian government. They were arrested but, as Hirohito must have observed, punished as the army thought appropriate – the toughest sentence being imposed on Colonel Hashimoto, who was locked up for less than two weeks.[2]

In 1932 fighting erupted in Shanghai, China's biggest trading city (a section of which was policed by the Japanese). Tensions caused by a

Chinese boycott of Japanese products led to clashes in the streets. The Imperial High Command authorized two divisions to be sent to Shanghai, Chinese forces retreated from the Japanese-controlled section of the city and a treaty ending the aggressive action was signed in May that year. While the fighting had raged in Shanghai two leading Japanese businessmen, known to be sympathetic to the notion of compromise with the West were assassinated in Japan. Shortly afterwards, prime minister Inukai, thought by many not to have supported the army sufficiently, was murdered as well. The effect of the military aggression on the mainland of Asia had been further to polarize political life in Japan and to leave the nationalists firmly in control.

The League of Nations condemned Japan's actions – and, predictably, the Japanese formally withdrew from the League in March 1933. Nothing illustrates better the contempt the Japanese leadership now had for the League than the fact that at the same moment the League was debating Japanese aggression in Manchukuo, the Imperial Army was advancing into the Chinese province of Jehol. The love affair between the Western democracies and Japan was over.

A propaganda film produced by the Imperial Army, *Japan in the National Emergency*, and shown in Japanese cinemas just months after the country withdrew from the League of Nations, demonstrates the prevailing nationalistic mood. 'In the past we have just followed the Western trend without thinking about it,' runs the commentary. 'As a result Japanese pride has faded away.... Today we are lucky to see the revival of the Japanese spirit throughout the nation.' In the film, corrupt Western values are personified by a young Japanese man who smokes a pipe and plays a mandolin, and by a Westernized young Japanese woman who smokes, dances and, in one of the film's most provocative tableaux, demands that a middle-aged Japanese man apologise when he inadvertently steps on her toe in the street. (The middle-aged man wears a beard in the style of the Emperor Meiji and is clearly intended to personify the strong authoritarian values that the late emperor possessed.) The mandolin-playing youth who accompanies the woman tries to demonstrate how the apology should be made – Western-style – by dropping to his knees and using his scarf to wipe her shoes clean. This is too much for the middle-aged man who pushes the youth aside to announce dramatically: 'Stupid! Listen to me! This is *Japan!*' The propaganda may be clumsy, but the message is clear. Women should return to their traditional subservient role and in the process reject smoking in public, Western-style clothes and standing up for themselves, whilst the Japanese as a whole should glory in their own uniqueness as a people. Japan should take technological knowledge from the Western democracies but reject the social and political values that the makers of the technology espouse. (Significantly, this film is regarded as still sufficiently sensitive in content that the Japanese archive house to which we traced a copy wished to censor its use and would not give the BBC permission to show contentious sections – fortunately, another copy of the film was traced in the National Archives in Washington.)

If Japan was to expand as the nationalists wished then crucial to future success was a large and powerful army. The growth of the Imperial Army during the first part of the twentieth century was phenomenal – by 1937 it was five times bigger than at the turn of the century. This kind of rapid expansion brought with it, unsurprisingly, problems for the military – chiefly, they worried about how to maintain discipline. They found one answer to the problem in the training of recruits, which became more brutal. If the soldiers made the smallest mistake they were physically beaten. 'Sometimes you'd be hit with fists, and sometimes you'd be hit with bamboo sticks,' says Toyoshige Karashima, who was then a Taiwanese recruit in the Imperial Army. 'Sometimes in the evening we couldn't eat our food because our faces were so swollen.' Another Japanese veteran, Masayo Enomoto, revealed that his instructors used to beat him and his fellow recruits so much during basic training that their arms ached, and by the day's end they had no energy left to hit them. As a consequence the instructors found a novel way of maintaining discipline – 'self-punishment': 'Once the instructors got tired of beating you up,' says Enomoto, 'they would have recruits face each other and slap each other. So we all of us recruits, comrades together, started to slap each other – instead of being slapped by the instructor. Gradually I felt that I'd missed out on something if by night-time I hadn't been beaten up at least once.' Hajime Kondo, another recruit into the Imperial Army, says simply that 'the training was so severe that I felt I'd rather die'.

The instructors hit the recruits with their fists, with bamboo canes, and hard across their faces with the heels of their boots. Significantly, the recruits were not just subjected to such beatings by those formally in command of them. Senior recruits also beat the more junior ones, especially in the early days of training while the new intake were struggling to pick up the specialized *argot* of the military. There was little hope of escaping harsh physical punishment – a whole section of soldiers would be beaten if one of their comrades failed in some way, the justification being that this was an attempt to instil in the recruits the sense that they were not individuals but part of a unit. It was institutionalized bullying. 'In the military there is no individual responsibility, only group responsibility,' says Hajime Kondo, who served in the Imperial Army in China. 'You're often punished not due to your own crime. At the very beginning I didn't think it was a good idea, but after a week, or a month or two, you learn that in the battlefield you have to behave as a group.'

Every single veteran we interviewed recalled an army training of the utmost brutality. The physical abuse of recruits was not arbitrary but planned and systematic, part of a carefully thought-out method by which the High Command attempted to mould the type of soldier they desired. When the recruit entered the Imperial Army he was joining a family – a cold, brutal family, but a family none the less. 'The barracks is the soldier's family where together soldiers share hardships and joys, life and death,' says the 1908 *Guntai naimusho* (army handbook).[3] 'A family means that the company is one household in the one village of the regiment. The heads of the household are the father and the mother. The company commander is a strict father, and the NCO a loving mother. The lieutenants are relatives and in perfect accord with their company commander whom they loyally assist.'

The sense of the regiment as one 'village' was further enhanced by each unit being recruited from only one area of Japan. Recruits would be surrounded by people with whom they had grown up. In such circumstances the pressure to conform and not 'disgrace' one's relatives back home must have been immense. Indeed, most of the veterans we interviewed confessed that their greatest fear was that by committing some misdemeanour in the army they might bring shame on their family.

Towering over the whole familial–hierarchical structure was the all-powerful god-figure of the emperor himself – the supreme commander of the imperial armed forces. The recruits had been taught since their schooldays that their emperor was a divine being, now through reciting the Imperial Rescript [proclamation] to Soldiers and Sailors, they learnt how much closer they were tied to the throne via their new status as soldiers in the emperor's personal army. They were told their equipment was given to them by the emperor – the barrel of their rifles carried the imperial chrysanthemum symbol – and every day recruits would bow in the direction of the Imperial Palace to show respect; each order they were given was issued 'in the name of the emperor'; every beating they received was meted out because the emperor would have wished it. Blind obedience to the emperor was the glue that held this ever-expanding army together.

With each passing year it became ever more apparent that the growing Imperial Army was being trained to fight and conquer China. In 1934, after taking Jehol Province, the Japanese moved on to Chahar and then as far as Hopei Province. The ostensible reason was to secure the protection of nearby Manchuria, but many in the Imperial Army had broader ambitions. The continuing tension between those factions in the army that wanted even more accelerated territorial expansion and those, chiefly politicians, who favoured securing existing gains, erupted in Tokyo on 26 February 1936. Soldiers of the Imperial Army in Tokyo – including the Third Imperial Guard Regiment – led by officers who were members of the far right 'Imperial Way' faction, moved during the night on those 'weak' government figures they despised. Viscount Saito, Lord Keeper of the Privy Seal, was murdered, as was General Watanabe, the newly appointed Inspector General of Military Education. Key buildings in the centre of Tokyo – the parliament building and the War Office amongst them – were seized. A pamphlet distributed by the revolution-

aries read: 'We have been compelled to annihilate those elder states-
men, military leaders, bureaucrats, political party leaders and other
criminals who have been shamelessly hindering the Heavenly prerogative of the Supreme Being....'[4]

But when the 'Supreme Being' heard about the rebellion he acted
with uncharacteristic steadfastness. Hirohito threatened to lead troops
against the plotters himself if his generals wavered. By 29 February the
rebellion was crushed. Universally lenient (or non-existent) punishments had been meted out to earlier conspirators, but this time thirteen
of the plotters were executed (though leading figures in the army fought
to minimize the number of officers who were arrested). The '2.26
Incident', as it is known in Japan, is significant for two reasons. It
demonstrated both that Hirohito had enormous latent power to control
events – power he very rarely chose to use – and that the Japanese military risked revolution from within if the policy of colonial expansion in
China was not pursued with sufficient radicalism.

In such unstable circumstances it needed only a spark to start a full-
scale war on the Asian mainland. And such a spark duly occurred.
Japanese troops were stationed in northern China to 'protect Japanese
interests' just as the British and Americans maintained a presence in
China at the time – since the Boxer rebellion forty years earlier, the
Chinese Nationalists, now under the leadership of Chiang K'ai-shek,
had been unable to prevent foreign governments placing troops on their
soil for 'protective' purposes. In July 1937, a Japanese force was conducting an exercise around the Hu River when the soldiers came to
what was known as the Marco Polo bridge. As they crossed it they
passed Chinese troops and a shot was fired, though who fired first has
never been conclusively established. The incident soon developed into a
minor battle. When the news reached Japan the mood was for war – the
Chinese must be taught a lesson. Three divisions were dispatched from
Japan, and on 27 July the Japanese airforce began to bomb Peking.

The war in China that began in July 1937 is infamous in the West
because of the brutal crimes that Japanese troops were to commit in
Nanking that December. But Nanking was part of a pattern set from the

early days of the conflict. From the first, Japanese troops were told that this was a war against sub-humans. 'We called the Chinese "*Chancorro*", says Yoshio Tshuchiya, who served in the Kempeitai, the infamous Japanese secret military police. '"*Chancorro*", that meant below human, like bugs or animals. Whereas the Japanese are a superior race, which had been in existence for 2600 years, the Chinese were inferior. The Chinese didn't belong to the human race. That was the way we looked at it.'

On arrival in China, soldiers of the Imperial Army were subject to additional training based on this theory that the enemy they were fighting were 'below human'. Hajime Kondo first learnt what this training would consist of when he and his comrades were summoned to a large, square, open area. On one side was a pit and next to it a mound of bodies. On the other side of the square, tied to trees, were Chinese men. 'We had no idea what was going on,' says Kondo. 'Then the boss said, "We are going to give you bayonet practice." We prepared our bayonets, and then two at a time we ran and we stabbed. When I first understood that we were killing them, stabbing live human beings, I was shaking. I was seventh or eighth to do it. At the order I ran and I stabbed and the bayonet went into the body very easily. I learnt that it was easy to bayonet a human being. We learnt it with our own hands. Once I did it, it became easy. I didn't think anything about the man I killed.'

Yoshio Tshuchiya underwent similar training in Manchuria. 'I didn't have courage at the beginning, but I couldn't escape from it. I would be labelled as "chicken". So I had to do it.' The first time he participated in this 'bayonet training' the victims were six Chinese men. 'I think they were farmers,' he says. 'They were not bandits or anti-Japanese.... Just some suspicious people who'd been caught.' Just like Hajime Kondo, Yoshio Tshuchiya found that once he had bayoneted one unarmed Chinaman it was easier to bayonet another: 'The first time you still have a conscience and feel bad. But if you are labelled as courageous, and honoured and given merit, and if you're praised as having this courage, that will be the driving power for the second time. If I'd thought of them as human beings I couldn't have done it. But because I thought of them as animals or below human beings, we did it.'

'I was taught that we should look down on the Chinese,' says Masayo

Enomoto, who also fought in the Imperial Army in Northern China. 'They were one rank lower than the Japanese and we should treat them as animals. This was something I was taught in the army and I believed it, and as a result we had a lot of evil.' Enomoto began his training in China by shooting prisoners. He and his comrades would tie Chinese men to poles and then use them as target practice. 'We tried to shoot the heart and I was successful, but my colleagues sometimes hit the abdomen and other parts of the body. They weren't very successful. So a single farmer could be shot by some ten or twenty people.' His emotional state as he shot these helpless human beings was simple: 'I felt like I was just killing animals, like pigs. And when the team leader asked who would like to go first I always raised my hand. And I thought that this was the way for the Japanese Imperial Army to do things. I was just totally convinced.'

Enomoto was an ambitious young man: ever since he had heard of the Japanese conquering Manchuria he had longed to make his fortune on the Asian mainland, and once he enlisted in the army he was keen to please. No matter what the task he wanted to be 'first in everything'. It was hardly surprising, then, that once he reached China he was soon promoted to junior NCO and military instructor. 'Even after I became an instructor my way of thinking didn't change at all,' he says. 'One time, when I was training my students, I brought in a Chinese farmer and I cut him with a big knife from his chest to his stomach. And I told the soldiers to look carefully at what I was doing. And I had to use some force because the knife wasn't that sharp. I cut this farmer and showed the young soldiers that the Chinese are beasts and that they had to do similar things.'

When Enomoto was pressed to explain why he thought this kind of behaviour was suitable 'training' for his recruits, he replied that there were no suitable 'educational tools' in the village other than the farmers. 'And I wanted to test the courage of the recruits,' he says. 'These soldiers had been in the military for six months and they were going to have to take part in a military operation for the first time in their lives, and I didn't have any other tools to educate them with. And the only thing I could think of was to kill someone in front of them and teach them what it's like to kill someone. And that's the reason I took that strategy.'

This was the kind of brutal training and conditioning that large numbers of Japanese soldiers received in China. Already their basic training had taught them that physical brutality was the appropriate response to the slightest setback, and now a belief that their enemy was 'below human' was added to the mix – a powerful cocktail that was to result in some of the most horrific war crimes committed in the twentieth century. The pre-condition for all the crimes committed by the Imperial Army in China was this belief beaten into the soldiers that the Chinese were inferior beings. The Japanese soldiers who had treated their German captives so well during the First World War had believed that these Westerners were at least their equals. After all, did not the West possess superior technology that the Japanese had had to discover and adapt for themselves? But as for the Chinese, the Japanese had looked down on them for centuries – nowhere better expressed than in the letter that Prince Shotoku of Japan had sent to the emperor of China hundreds of years before: Shotoku had called the Chinese emperor 'Emperor of the Setting Sun' and signed himself 'Emperor of the Rising Sun.'[5]

To the Japanese, China appeared ripe for conquest. Ever since the revolution of 1911 the country had been riven by internal conflict. Central government was weak – in some places non-existent. Warlords fought for control of some provinces, others were dominated either by the fledgling Chinese Communists under Mao Tse-Tung or the Chinese Nationalists under Chiang K'ai-shek. In the words of the historian J. M. Roberts, 'it was a little like the end of the Roman Empire'.

As they fought their way towards the then capital of China, Nanking, Japanese troops left a trail of brutality behind them. In the city of Suchow on the banks of the Tai Hu Lake, for example, they raped and murdered to such a degree that, according to the *Chinese Weekly Review*, only 500 people were left in the city out of a pre-war population of 350,000.[6] Thousands were left for dead, many more fled and hid in the countryside.

The Japanese army finally reached Nanking in December 1937. After a brief struggle the defences collapsed and on 13 December the invading force swept into the city. Instantly, many captured Chinese soldiers were simply murdered. Masatake Okumiya was one of the first Japanese naval officers to arrive in Nanking and witnessed the executions of several hundred Chinese soldiers: 'They didn't make any noise, they were very quiet. They were tied with their hands behind their back. They were lined up by the river bank and bayonets and swords were used for killing them. Then they were thrown in the river. First I was very shocked, surprised. But because of the atmosphere I gradually got used to it. In the end I didn't think about it. I didn't feel anything about it. I was just looking at it. And since I was a naval officer I was not in a position to intrude into an army affair.'

It was not just captured soldiers who were savagely treated by the Japanese – women and children were at risk too. There were a substantial number of Westerners in Nanking and many bore witness to the atrocities committed on civilians within the city after its surrender. 'On the night of December 14 there were many cases of Japanese soldiers entering Chinese houses and raping women or taking them away,'[7] wrote Lewis Smythe, Secretary of the International Committee for the Nanking Safety Zone. 'We Europeans are paralysed with horror,' recorded John Rabe, Chairman of the International Committee for the Nanking Safety Zone. 'There are executions everywhere, some are being carried out with machine guns outside the barracks of the War Ministry. Last night up to 1000 women and girls were said to have been raped. About 100 girls in Ginling college alone. You hear of nothing but rape. If husbands or brothers intervene, they're shot.'[8] 'The slaughter of civilians is appalling,' said Dr Robert Wilson of the International Red Cross. 'Rape and brutality almost beyond belief. Two girls aged about 16 were raped to death in one of the refugee camps. In the University Middle School, where there are over 8000 people the Japs came in ten times last night, over the wall, stole food, clothing and raped until they were satisfied. They bayoneted one little boy, killing him, and I spent an hour and a half this morning patching up another little boy of eight who had five bayonet wounds.'[9]

Xiuying Li was nineteen years old when the Japanese army arrived in Nanking. She was seven months pregnant, and her husband had left the city days before. He thought it would be too dangerous for his wife to accompany him and he believed that women and children left within the city would be safe. Surely the Japanese would not molest his pregnant wife? But on the morning of 19 December Japanese soldiers broke into the house where she was hiding. Xiuying Li had already seen other women dragged into a nearby house to be raped and, since she saw none of them emerge afterwards, probably killed. 'The soldiers came into our room,' she says. 'I knew if they dragged me into that house then I would also die. So I bumped my head into the wall and became unconscious. And several women were taken by the Japanese. After they left, some older women comforted me. They put me onto a bed. At that time I began to think – I want to die, but I didn't die.' As she lay in bed she resolved to try to fight the Japanese soldiers when they came back – even if it meant her own death. Later that day, once it was dark, the Japanese returned. 'There was one soldier who saw me and he began to drive the other women out of the room. And he came for me. He wasn't as tall as me and I began to bite him. I was very angry. I said that Japanese could not be called human beings. He began to shout and two other Japanese soldiers came and they began to bayonet me. I got lots of wounds in my face and lots of blood came out. Then I became unconscious and they thought I had died and they left.'

Xiuying Li's father returned home to find what he believed was the dead body of his daughter. Only when he took her outside into the cold air to bury her did he realize that she was not dead, but unconscious. Immediately he took her to the nearby foreign hospital where she was treated for multiple stab wounds. On her second day in hospital she lost the baby boy she was carrying. As she lay in her hospital bed her father told her that their home had been burnt down 'because Japanese soldiers wanted to get warm and set up lots of fires, and they didn't care about the houses'.

A few days later, an American missionary, the Reverend John Magee, brought a home movie camera into the hospital and took pictures of the victims. The significance of this film footage of the injured Xiuying Li would only become apparent years later when its existence became known in Japan. Incredibly, one writer on the ultra-right in Japan recently denied that the Xiuying Li in the film was the one who exists today. On the face of it, it is a nonsensical claim. Not only are there witnesses alive in Nanking today who have known Xiuying Li all her life (including the nurse who treated her in the hospital at the time) but the most cursory glance at her face today, sixty-four years later, shows multiple scar wounds. Through lawyers in Japan Xiuying Li is pursuing a libel action against the writer concerned. But, understandably, she feels that this allegation is another crime against her. The attempt by some in Japan to discredit survivors of the Nanking massacre (even to deny that the massacre ever happened) is a phenomenon that has not received the publicity it deserves in the West – it is as if a substantial body of opinion in Germany sought to allege that Holocaust victims were simply 'making it up', for this attempt to downplay what Japanese soldiers did in Nanking is not confined to the lunatic fringe. There is a lively debate in Japan over the number of people killed in the Nanking massacre. Most Western estimates are that several hundred thousand died, but at least one respected Japanese professor maintains the number is in the low tens of thousands. Significantly, those Japanese academics who seek to minimise the number of Chinese dead often omit from their writings any detailed mention of the crimes committed or any sense of national shame about what happened in Nanking. More than once on my research trips to Japan I heard the phrase, often uttered by eminent people, that 'the Japanese did nothing in the war to apologise for'.

The Nanking massacre remains by far the most infamous of Japanese crimes in China. As a result, there has been considerable debate as to how such an atrocity could have occurred. Contributing factors suggested by various historians include the frustration felt by Japanese troops who had been forced to battle hard in the preceding weeks to conquer Shanghai, a city they had optimistically expected to take in a matter of days, and the notion that the Imperial Army were 'rewarded' for their achievement in taking the Nationalists' capital by being permitted to rape and murder with impunity.

However, such explanations will only ever be part of the truth, because focusing on particular reasons for the Nanking massacre implies that what happened there in 1937 was wholly out of the ordinary. And whilst it is true that in terms of scale the atrocity was unique amongst

Japanese war crimes, what's often missed, especially in the West, is that in terms of type Nanking was not extraordinary at all. Seen in the context of Japanese beliefs about the Chinese, and the training of Japanese troops at the time, the events at Nanking become all too understandable.

Take, for example, the attitude of Japanese soldiers to Chinese women. Horrific stories are told of the rape of young girls and old women in Nanking. Gang rapes followed by the murder of the victims were almost commonplace. There's even anecdotal evidence of Japanese soldiers tearing open the stomachs of pregnant women and bayoneting the foetuses. But Japanese soldiers did not suddenly start to rape and mistreat Chinese women only when they reached Nanking. The problem had been all too evident five years earlier when, during the Shanghai incident in January 1932, soldiers of the Imperial Army committed a whole series of rapes. So serious was the problem in Shanghai that senior army officers decided to adopt a radical solution proposed by General Okamura Yausji, deputy chief of staff of the Shanghai Expeditionary Army – they would establish and run brothels for their men in order to dissuade them from raping the general population. Japanese soldiers would not need to look for sex – the army would provide it for them.

Initially the idea was that Japanese prostitutes would staff the military brothels, but the army soon changed its policy and began to search for women from elsewhere within their empire, especially when many more 'comfort stations' were established in the wake of the atrocities at Nanking. But, as became immediately apparent, there were not enough willing volunteers. The Imperial Army solved that problem in a straightforward, brutal way – if women would not become prostitutes willingly, they would be tricked or forced into prostitution. The experience of Sol Shinto, recruited as a teenager in Korea, is typical. She was approached in the remote village where she lived and asked if she would like to take a job working for the Japanese army, cleaning the barracks and washing the soldiers' uniforms. Coming as she did from a desperately poor background, she saw this as an opportunity both to make money and to 'serve the country' (like all Koreans at the time, she had been taught that she was a subject of the Japanese emperor – Korea had formally been under

Japanese control since 1910). She was taken to a camp in northern China where she learnt that she had been recruited not as a cleaner or washer-woman, but as a prostitute. 'I was told that I had to "take care" of the sol-diers,' says Shinto. 'Of course professional women, prostitutes, know how to do this, but I didn't know. I was very naïve. I was sixteen years old.' When she heard that this was to be her job she was horrified, but, hundreds of miles from home and penniless, she had no means of escape. When she protested that she had been tricked into prostitution, she was slapped and told once more that she would have to 'take care' of the sol-diers. 'I was told I'd just have to lie on the bed, that's all you do. Then the men, the soldiers would come in. But it's not just lying on the bed, is it?' From the first she found the experience of having sex with Japanese sol-diers 'very painful'. She spoke little Japanese and the soldiers spoke hardly any Korean, so at the start she could barely communicate with them. 'I had to be obedient,' she says. 'And if I was not then I would be slapped. Many battalions would come along and sometimes it would be very busy, and I think occasionally I would black out. Sometimes there would be perhaps seventy soldiers a day, from seven in the morning until twelve at night. It was very busy, fifteen or twenty minutes per man, and then the other people queuing up behind. I might be told to get totally naked, nude, and people wanted to take photographs. And I was told to take many positions, on top. That was tough. But if I said no then the sol-diers would slap me and demand, "Why are you in the brothel in the first place?" I mean, I couldn't talk Japanese, I couldn't answer back in Japanese. And there were violent officers who would rampage around. So really I was just trying to find somewhere to die.'

As a comfort woman Sol Shinto was a creature the soldiers of the Imperial Army could treat as they wished. Known as 'public toilets', comfort women were often at risk of severe physical violence. Once one of the soldiers drew his sword in front of Shinto. Drunk, he lashed around and cut her back – she still bears the scar to this day. Another sol-dier, who took a particular fancy to her, demanded that she have her Japanese name tattooed on her arm. She complied with an abject sense of resignation, thinking that this too must be just another 'part of the job'.

Some of the soldiers who had sex with her grew fond of Shinto and, in a request that offers insight into the suffering they themselves were enduring at the time, asked her if she would 'commit suicide' with them. 'When I was asked if I would commit suicide with them I always refused,' she says. 'If you die you die, and can't be revived.' She learnt first hand how 'some soldiers were deaf and hard of hearing, some were near blind, because of all the slapping, the violence they went through. I could see some soldiers who were hit and who were really bullied by the other soldiers, and I saw one Japanese soldier who actually committed suicide by diving into a pond.'

For all this suffering, for enduring all this horrific treatment, Sol Shinto was paid a salary of precisely nothing by the manager of the military brothel she worked in. 'I got pocket money sometimes from the soldiers and the officers,' she told us. 'But I never got any wages.'

There is no exact figure for how many 'comfort women' (though 'victims of forced rape' is a more accurate term) were employed and abused by the Japanese in this way. Estimates range from 80,000 to 100,000. But the overall scale of the crime is clear, as is the complicity of the Imperial Army and Japanese government of the time. In the words of Professor Yuki Tanaka, who has made a special study of Japanese policy towards comfort women: 'The comfort women case could well be historically unprecedented as an instance of state controlled criminal activity involving the sexual exploitation of women.'[11]

Moreover, if the purpose of the 'comfort stations' was to prevent Japanese soldiers raping Chinese women, then the policy was a spectacular failure – not just because of the infamous events in Nanking, but because of the subsequent behaviour of Japanese troops during the war against China, particularly in what became known as the Sanko 'pacification' actions in the north of the country. Hajime Kondo took part in the Sanko actions and paints an astonishing picture of the mentality of the Japanese soldiers who fought in this brutal struggle. 'We had the feeling that in the enemy district we could do anything,' he says. 'We were not told officially we could do anything but we learnt it from our senior colleagues. Basically it was all connected to the emperor system.

We were brought up to kill communists and in this province everybody was communist so these people should all be killed for the emperor. That was the thinking of the ordinary soldiers.'

This attitude of 'kill all the communists' is reminiscent of the behaviour of German troops in the war against the Soviet Union which began in 1941. Hitler had declared that Germany's war in the East was to be a 'different kind' of war from that fought in the West. The war in the East was to be a war of 'annihilation' against 'sub-humans'. And the parallels do not end there: to anyone who has heard German veterans speak about their attacks on Russian villages suspected of concealing 'partisans', the testimony of Masayo Enomoto, who served in the Imperial Army in China, sounds chillingly familiar: 'When you enter a village, first you steal their valuables. Then you kill people and then you set the village on fire and burn everything. Such killing, burning and robbing was seen everywhere.'

However, there is one glaring respect in which the Japanese soldiers behaved differently from their German allies. Whilst both Germans and Japanese raped women in the territories they occupied, the Imperial Army committed the crime on a far greater scale. German rape of Russian women was against explicit Nazi racial teaching, but the Japanese had no such racial 'scruples' when it came to sex and it appears that any Chinese woman was fair game. Enomoto was one Japanese soldier who freely confessed he had committed rape during his time in China. 'We'd go into villages as part of the operations, singly or together, and then if we saw any women in the village we would rape them. And if there were two of us, then one would keep guard and we wouldn't talk about it afterwards.' On occasion Enomoto did not choose to rape the women he found – he chose to torture them instead. Once, in the countryside looking for Chinese soldiers, he and his comrades came upon 'a woman who was about twenty-seven or twenty-eight. We had some petrol and we covered her in it and set fire to her so she died.' When asked to explain how it was possible that he could do such a thing, he replied: 'We were going to battle and we thought we were probably going to die, so it's a strange word to use but I think we were looking for some sort of entertainment.'

After the war, Enomoto was one of the few Japanese soldiers held to account for their actions, imprisoned first by the Russians and then by the Chinese. And once he had fallen into the hands of his enemies one wartime crime in particular returned to haunt him. 'I went into this village and there was a girl aged about fifteen there. And I went up to her, and then her father appeared, so I killed him. I wanted to rape her and so I thought, well, if he was her father he probably wouldn't be very happy if I was raping his daughter, so I shot him. I didn't have very long to do it all in. As I said, I'd just arrived in the village. She cried and she was shaking. She may have known what was going to happen to her and she was shaking. So then I raped her and killed her there and then after raping her. But what happened was that there was a young boy who caused me problems later. He was hiding and I thought he was just a young child so I thought it would be OK, but when the war trials took place he appeared and he recognized me, and that led to problems for me.' Astonishingly, the Chinese did not execute confessed murderers and rapists like Masayo Enomoto after the war. Instead, in the late 1950s they allowed them to return to Japan. (One consequence of this policy is that veterans like him are free to speak of their crimes without risk of further prosecution.)

Enomoto's crimes are terrible indeed, but the most shocking part of his interview was the moment when he was asked about his own sense of guilt:

'During the operations there were many times when you raped women. Did you not feel guilty about what you were doing?'

'I didn't feel any sense of guilt then,' he replied.

'Why? Why didn't you have any sense of guilt then?'

'Because I was fighting for the emperor. He was a god. In the name of the emperor we could do whatever we wanted against the Chinese. Therefore I had no sense of guilt.'

Time and again when we pressed Japanese veterans to explain similar acts of barbarism or cruelty they would respond in the same way. 'We were doing it for the emperor – he was a god,' became as familiar an exculpatory phrase as the German 'We were acting under orders.' In a way, such an attempt to escape individual culpability is understandable. These Japanese soldiers had been trained never to think for themselves – only to show unquestioning loyalty through their NCOs and officers to the emperor himself. They had been taught that every military operation they took part in was for the glory of their sacred emperor.

Hajime Kondo, who during the Sanko 'pacification' actions believed that 'if you kill a person then it's good for the emperor', also has powerful memories of the atrocities he and his colleagues committed against women and children. 'When soldiers went into the village and entered the houses, they first searched for any valuables to take, then they searched for women,' he says. 'Once, my comrades found a woman in her thirties and then a group rape took place. Normally when group rape happened the victims were killed. But this time she and her baby were not killed but taken with us to the next base camp. Then she was taken with us on the march the next day.' The woman was stripped, and made to march over mountainous territory naked apart from her shoes. Kondo believes her clothes were taken from her because this made it difficult for her to escape, but it is hard to believe that the soldiers were not also motivated by a desire to cause further sexual humiliation to the poor woman.

During a break in the march Kondo heard older soldiers whispering 'What should we do?' as both the woman and her child were clearly becoming weaker. 'Suddenly one of the soldiers stood up,' he says, 'and grabbed her baby and threw it over a cliff which was thirty to forty metres high. Then instantly the mother of the baby followed, jumping off the cliff. And when I saw what was happening in front of me I thought what a horrible thing to do. I felt sorry for them for a while, but I had to carry on marching.'

Whilst the murder of a small child in this way may not have been a frequent occurrence, the crime of rape, as we have seen, was commonplace – so much so that the rigid system of hierarchy within the Imperial Army, with the senior soldiers bullying the more junior, was even carried over into the way the abuse of the Chinese women was conducted. 'Rookies were too tired to rape,' says Kondo. 'The rookies were treated so badly, made to carry heavy loads, and the other soldiers were so mean to us, that I could never think of women.' But in an admission of startling honesty, he confessed that once he was deemed 'senior' enough he too was invited to participate in group rape. 'The soldiers caught a woman and one by one they committed rape. And I was in my third year as a soldier and one of the fourth-year soldiers summoned me and said, "Kondo, you go and rape." You couldn't turn it down.'

The insight offered by Hajime Kondo's description of the circumstances surrounding the rape he committed is significant, for it demonstrates the institutionalized nature of the crime. For these Japanese soldiers, rape had become more than an act of sexual violence; it had become a kind of bonding exercise between comrades, a reward to be offered to junior soldiers once they had proved their worth. Military training is built around acts of initiation, the receiving of symbolic rewards like a beret once a difficult period of training has been completed. Clearly, for the soldiers in Hajime Kondo's unit, and probably for many thousands of other soldiers in the Imperial Army fighting in China, being invited to participate in a group rape became just such an act of initiation – a demonstration by the senior members of the squad that after years of training a junior soldier was finally thought worthy of truly 'belonging' to the unit.

Officially, rape was a crime in the Japanese army. But only a handful of those who committed the offence were ever held to account for their actions, not only because many of the soldiers killed their victims after the crime, but also because senior officers must have either turned a blind eye to what was happening or indeed condoned it. A similar situation occurred during the training of recruits, where much of the brutal bullying and punishment was administered not 'officially' by the NCOs or officers, but by other more senior soldiers of the same rank. Professor Edward Drea makes an insightful comparison with political parties in Japan, who use 'go betweens' (in Japanese *nakadachi*) 'to deal with unsavory elements that the politicians cannot officially have links with for reasons of avoiding confrontations and maintaining group solidarity'.[12] Thus it is simply not accurate, as some Japanese apologists claim, that the rapes encouraged in this institutionalized way by senior soldiers within each squad were the actions of men going against firm orders that preached the contrary. From the moment they entered training the recruits learnt first to fear the more senior members of the squad and then to imitate them. This was the only way they could avoid entering an ever-increasing spiral of vicious bullying. Just as no sane recruit would have complained to an officer about being bullied by a more senior soldier, so it would have been rash in the extreme for a relatively junior soldier like Hajime Kondo to refuse to take part in a group rape when finally asked to do so. And it seems likely, since so very few of those Japanese soldiers who committed such crimes were ever punished for them by the Japanese army, that the senior soldiers within the units who initiated these group rapes must have known that, tacitly at least, their superior officers would not be particularly concerned at their actions. A Japanese officer in such a case would (as Emperor Hirohito was to try to do after the war) first and foremost seek to preserve credible 'deniability'. The system was best served by those higher up the hierarchy trying *not* to find out if their men were raping anyone.

All of which leads to the central question – given his phenomenal importance to his troops, how much did Hirohito know about the brutal way his army was conducting the war in China? This is a profoundly sensitive question to ask in Japan and one that has been made deliberately hard to answer. Documents that might conclusively establish the truth have either been destroyed or are still kept secret. In the weeks following their surrender thousands of documents were burnt by the Japanese before the Americans arrived to occupy their country. Thousands more are still kept hidden in Japanese archives. So in the absence of incontestable evidence, historians have been forced to speculate. Take, for example, Hirohito's state of knowledge about the Nanking massacre. For Edward Behr, one of Hirohito's first critical biographers, 'it is difficult to believe that this – one of the most appalling events of the China War – came and went without Emperor Hirohito becoming aware of it'. Behr points out both that Prince Asaka, one of the Japanese commanders in Nanking, was Hirohito's own grand-uncle, and that Hirohito would surely have been aware of coverage of the massacre in the foreign press. Stephen Large, in his measured biography of Hirohito, is less certain, demonstrating that Hirohito relied primarily on the information others chose to give him in order to form his own views. Herbert Bix, in the latest full-length examination of the emperor, leans more towards the Behr view – that it is virtually inconceivable that Hirohito did not know about Nanking at the time.

Trying to decide what Hirohito knew overall about the criminal conduct of his troops in China is like peeling away the layers of an onion, only to reach the core and find nothing there. This, of course, is precisely the difficulty that those around him hoped future historians would encounter. The 'deniability' of the emperor must always have been the paramount concern of his advisers. But despite this carefully constructed wall of vagueness, it is still possible to reach definite conclusions about Hirohito's culpability. For it is certain that at some point he would have known of the crimes his army had committed – even if it was only from the Americans at the end of the war (and it would have been truly extraordinary if he did not know sooner than that). Yet at no time in his long life did Hirohito call for those who had committed crimes in China to be investigated and properly held to account for their actions. His silence, in fact, is hugely eloquent. As supreme commander of the imperial armed forces he was ultimately responsible for the actions of his soldiers – a man of honour who held such a position would, no matter at what stage he learnt the truth, have openly admitted and publicized his country's culpability and wanted those who were guilty to be punished. Instead, Hirohito's actions are entirely consistent with those of a head of state who wanted his army to succeed and was indifferent to the methods they used to do it – a philosophy reminiscent of one of Hitler's orders to his subordinates, when he told them to 'Germanize Poland, and he would ask no questions about their methods'.

One of Hirohito's most important functions in the Japanese constitutional system was to question his military commanders about the methods his army was using – no one else, least of all the civilian cabinet, was in a position to do so. And yet Hirohito either knew what his army was doing and did nothing about it, or deliberately did not ask the questions that needed to be asked in order to find out. It is hard to know which is worthy of greater moral condemnation.

Moreover, Professor Bix reveals that in certain key areas Hirohito was clearly involved in a military decision-making process that led in China to the use of outlawed weapons. In a directive dated 28 July 1937 Hirohito sanctioned the use of tear gas in China (banned under the Versailles peace treaty signed by the Japanese at the end of the First World War), and two months later he authorized 'special chemical war-fare units' to be sent to the Asian mainland.[13] The Imperial Army went on to use poison gas on many hundreds of occasions during the war in China – the ultimate authorization for their actions coming from direc-tives sealed by their emperor. Such internationally outlawed weapons were never used in the subsequent war against the West – a revealing distinction that speaks of the pragmatism of the emperor and his mili-tary advisers (since they must have been concerned about the Western Allies using similar weapons against them in reprisal) rather than any sudden moral scruple.

Whilst documents tie Hirohito to knowledge of the use of chemical weapons by the Imperial Army in China, the paper chain does not con-clusively establish his guilt in the use of bacteriological weapons, though it is clear that he must have at least read some of the documents relating to the infamous Unit 731, Japan's biological warfare research unit. Under General Ishii, Unit 731 provided assistance to the conventional forces of the Imperial Army in China by such methods as 'infected-rat air-raids' in which rats contaminated with plague and other toxins were dropped on the Chinese. A measure of how deadly this bizarre and hor-rific weapon could be is that once, when the rats were dropped in the wrong place, 1600 Japanese troops became infected and died.[14] The Japanese use of bacteriological weapons during the conflict on the Asian mainland and their policy of testing these weapons first on innocent Chinese is one of the darkest crimes of the twentieth century.

An insight into the mentalities of those Japanese who took part in these human medical experiments in China is given by Ken Yuasa, a

Japanese doctor who worked in a military hospital in Shansi prefecture in China – a hospital visited many times by General Ishii, director of Unit 731. Yuasa was posted to the hospital after receiving a similar education to that of the other veterans interviewed. He was taught that 'all the subjects of the nation should serve the emperor and dedicate their lives to the emperor and die for him. That's what we were told. To dedicate our lives for the emperor so as to pay the debt we owed our parents.' Similarly, Yuasa believed that it was necessary to seek expansion on the Asian mainland so that 'Japan could become an imperial power – to become a big and great country, like the Western countries'. If, during his education or his subsequent service as a doctor in Asia, he ever felt the remotest desire to question the prevailing *mores* he always knew that, 'if you made any criticism, even among friends, that was a really frightening thing. Because if you did that you'd be scolded by your military superior or your teacher, and called a "non-patriot". It's probably difficult for the younger generation to understand just what that would mean. It's like excommunication from your village or community. It's probably more severe than if you had committed a crime.' Dr Yuasa finally arrived in China having learnt that the 'Chinese and Koreans were like waste and garbage'.

About six weeks after he began work in the military hospital the general manager approached him and said there would be an 'operations exercise' that evening and told Dr Yuasa to attend. 'I felt very uneasy, but, of course, I couldn't say anything. In the military, orders are absolute.' Dr Yuasa was anxious because he knew that in order to train doctors to become surgeons quickly the Japanese army was organizing 'practice' operations on healthy Chinese. As he walked into the operating theatre he saw two Chinese men standing against the wall. One was 'taller than me, well built, around thirty. The other was forty to fifty years old, he looked like a farmer. He was crying.'

The younger Chinese moved forward when he was ordered to and lay on the operating table. The older man resisted and Dr Yuasa went over and helped push him towards a second operating table in the room. 'I had never beaten anyone before, but because of my military indoctrination I was able to push him. I still remember, I held my feet strongly on the ground and pushed and then the farmer gave up and went forward. We had to demonstrate our greatness in front of the Korean soldiers [considered 'inferior' members of the Imperial Army] who were there. Then I was very proud.' Once on the operating table the farmer was forcibly injected with anaesthetic and then the 'operation' began. 'One of the doctors punched the farmer's thigh – that meant the anaesthetic was working. The first operation was removing an appendix because there were many appendix cases amongst Japanese soldiers – we didn't have any antibiotics and there were quite a few cases of soldiers dying as a result of that operation. The medical officer doing this operation was not very experienced and a healthy appendix is quite slippery, so I think he had to make the incision three times. After that his intestine was removed, then his arms were amputated and then the doctor practised injecting him in his heart.' Right to the end of this gruesome procedure the farmer kept breathing until 'eventually another officer and myself tried to hold his neck' whilst he was injected with the drugs that finally killed him. After the middle-aged farmer died, the younger Chinese was assaulted in a similar way. Altogether, during his time in China, Dr Yuasa participated in around six of these human vivisection experiments at his hospital on a total of ten healthy Chinese men. None of the victims survived.

Dr Yuasa and his colleagues always used general anaesthetic on their Chinese victims, but elsewhere the Japanese conducted human experiments without anaesthetic of any kind. Once, at another Japanese military hospital in China, Dr Yuasa attended a lecture and suddenly heard the head of the medical division announce, 'I will show you something good'. He took them to the nearby prison, and there, in front of the assembled doctors, two Chinese men were shot in the abdomen so that the Japanese could 'practise removing the bullet' in field conditions, without anaesthetic. 'I think they died of great pain during that operation,' says Dr Yuasa. 'I still remember their sort of cry, but I didn't pay much attention because we actually treated them as materials – we called them *maruta* ['timber' or 'logs'].'

Doctors like Ken Yuasa murdered Chinese during conventional operations. At his research camp in Manchuria General Ishii (and later

Kitano Masaji) of Unit 731 killed the local population in more advanced experiments. As Sheldon Harris, who has conducted ground-breaking work into the activities of Unit 731, recorded:

> 'They researched human reactions to plague, typhoid, paratyphoid A and B, typhus, smallpox, tularemia, infectious jaundice, gas gangrene, tetanus, cholera, dysentery, glanders, scarlet fever, undulant fever, tick encephalitis, 'songo' or epidemic hemorrhagic fever, whooping cough, diphtheria, pneumonia, berysipelas, epidemic cerebrospinal meningitis, venereal diseases, tuberculosis, salmonella, frostbite, and countless other diseases that were endemic to the communities and surrounding regions that fell within the responsibility of a Unit 731 branch Water Purification Unit. No one has been able to catalogue completely all the maladies that the various death factories in Manchuria visited on human guinea pigs.'[15]

Horrific stories like this emphasize how impossible it is to overestimate the atmosphere of cruelty in which the Japanese conducted their war in China. The context of this war would, in turn, contribute to the brutal storm that broke upon Allied servicemen once the Pacific War began. Indeed, probably the greatest single Western misconception about the war against the Japanese is that it began, for all parties, in December 1941 with the bombing of Pearl Harbor. For the Japanese, the war against the Western Allies was but a part of their overall struggle for supremacy in Asia, a conflict that had begun in Manchuria. For the Imperial Army, the war in Asia lasted from 1931 to 1945 – it was not merely the four-year struggle against the Western nations that began in 1941.

Thus it is a grave mistake to try to understand why the Japanese behaved as they did in the Pacific War without understanding the conditioning that soldiers of the Imperial Army received during the war in China that both preceded it and then carried on alongside it. At the turn of the twenty-first century, particularly since the publication of Joanna Bourke's intriguing work *An Intimate History of Killing*, it has become fashionable to emphasize how much men can *enjoy* killing – and there is clearly much insight to be gained by shining a light on to this darker side of the male psyche. But the revelation that throughout history men have taken pleasure in combat does not ultimately help us to understand how a nation that behaved so well to its prisoners in the First World War was, less than twenty years later, using its captives for bayonet practice and human experiments. One answer to this paradox lies in knowledge of how the German army behaved during the Second World War. After the war in the Soviet Union began in June 1941, there were some units that served first in the West, then in the East and then back in the West again. Interviews with veterans who went back and forth like this demonstrate that it was possible for the same soldier to behave 'chivalrously' in the West and then bestially in the East. The identical unit could happily treat prisoners with respect in the West, yet shoot their captives without remorse in the East. And the reason they could behave in such a schizo-phrenic way was their contrasting beliefs about their enemies. In western Europe they faced nations who they believed were 'civilized', whilst in the East they confronted a 'Judeo–Bolshevik' mass of 'subhumans'.

All of which leads to the inescapable conclusion that the overwhelm-ing reason that the Japanese treated the Chinese so badly was that they believed them to be utterly inferior – mere 'beasts'. And whilst the Japanese rapidly discovered that defeating these 'beasts' was going be tougher than they had thought (Hitler also underestimated the Red Army, to his cost), which led to frustration, which led to still greater brutality, it remains the case that the pre-condition without which these appalling crimes could not have been committed was the Japanese loathing of the Chinese which preceded the war.

During the 1930s, while the Japanese conducted their barbarous campaign in Asia, both the Western democracies and the emerging Western fascist states debated how best to deal with this growing Asian super-power. How they chose to react to the Japanese aggression was to be a crucial reason why the Pacific War occurred when it did. It is a story of racism, military incompetence and overweening self-confidence – and is the subject of Chapter 2.

DEALING WITH THE WEST

By taking control of Manchuria in 1931 the Japanese solved one pressing problem – the need for 'living space'; but they created another – the antagonism of the Western democracies. The call of the hard-line militarists for Japan to throw off all contact with the West may have been seductive, but it was impractical. Japan had few natural resources of its own and relied largely on oil imports from the United States to fuel not just the Imperial Army but the whole commercial operation of the country. Japan simply did not possess the raw materials necessary to endure total isolation in the modern machine age. Yet from the moment that the Imperial Army took Manchuria it was politically inconceivable that the Japanese would give up their new-found Garden of Eden. But without compromise over Manchuria, the anger of the West could not be calmed. Resolving these contradictory positions without eventual armed conflict was, from the first, a delicate and problematic task given the suspicion and distrust that existed on all sides.

The prevailing view of many in the Japanese elite was expressed by Prince Fumimaro Konoe, who was to be prime minister three times before the end of the war. For years Konoe had been calling on Japan to reject what he took to be the hypocritical values of the Western democracies. In an essay written in 1933, he condemned Western nations who

'brandish the Covenant of the League of Nations and, holding high the No-War treaty as their shield, censure us! Some of them even go as far as to call us public enemies of peace or humanity! Yet it is they, not we, who block world peace. They are not qualified to judge us.... As a result of our one million annual population increase, our national economic life is extremely burdened. We cannot wait for a rationalising adjustment of the world system. Therefore we have chosen to advance into Manchuria and Mongolia as our only means of survival.'[1]

It was Neville Chamberlain who, during 1933 and 1934 (years before he became infamous as the appeaser of Hitler), first mooted one possible solution – the recognition of the Japanese puppet state of Manchukuo in exchange for 'a permanent friendship with Japan.'[2] There was no consensus in the British cabinet for such a dramatic diplomatic step, and the plan was dropped. This strangled initiative is significant for two reasons: it shows that Chamberlain personally was prepared to appease not just the Nazis but the Japanese, and it demonstrated the willingness of British politicians to discuss possible solutions to the problem of Japanese expansion outside the unified approach of the League of Nations.

There were officials in the State Department in Washington who favoured a similar rapprochement with Japan over Manchuria, but they were outnumbered by those who either thought that such a policy would only encourage greater Japanese aggression in Asia or (and this group included the new President, Franklin Roosevelt) did not wish to be overly 'distracted' by events in China from the urgent task of rebuilding the economy and dragging the United States from the Depression. This unwillingness to engage with the problems caused by Japan's isolation from the League of Nations is symbolized by US behaviour at the naval disarmament conference which opened in London in 1935 – no agreement of any sort was reached with Japan and it was assumed that the early raft of naval treaties, outlining the extent to which each country's navy could grow relative to the other, had simply lapsed.

In 1936 the attitude of the Japanese government and military hardened in the wake of the rebellion of February of that year. In August two documents, *The Fundamentals of National Policy* and *Foreign Policy Guidelines*,[3] for the first time named the United States and Britain as possible enemies, along with the Soviet Union and China. The basic assumption of both these documents, discussed and approved by the

Japanese cabinet, was that Japan must maintain its position on the Asian mainland, defend itself from any possible threat from the Soviet Union to the north, and, at some uncertain point in the future, try to obtain more territory in the Pacific. At first sight this list of priorities represents confidence verging on hubris within the Japanese ruling class. How could one small nation hope to defy both of its giant neighbours, China and the Soviet Union, whilst also stating as a foreign policy goal further expansion to the east and south? The truth is that these foreign policy documents were an attempt to paper over differences that were still not resolved within the Japanese military. One faction thought that the greatest threat to Japan was posed by the Soviet Union; another, predominantly the Imperial Navy, believed that the lapsing of the naval treaties (which had restricted the expansion of the fleet) meant that the priority should be to solve Japan's problems by moving out into the Pacific.

Although these fundamental questions about Japan's potential enemies remained unresolved, there was consensus within the Japanese government and military as to which country was their greatest potential friend – Nazi Germany. Both countries had in the early 1930s turned their back on democracy; both felt cheated by those older Western nations that had seized colonies in the eighteenth and nineteenth centuries and now, hypocritically as they saw it, denied newer nations the chance to do the same; both countries were rearming at a frantic pace; both countries felt threatened by the Soviet Union and by the creed of communism, and crucially, whilst both dreamt of expansion their territorial ambitions did not clash. It was natural, then, that Japan joined an 'anti-Comintern Pact' (an alliance against the spread of communism) with Germany in November 1936, thus demonstrating to the world that her strongest friends in the West were the new fascist nations of Germany and Italy.

By June 1937, with the fall of prime minister Hayashi and the appointment of Prince Fumimaro Konoe in his place, the fissure that divided Japan from the Western democracies grew all but unbridgeable. Liberated, as he saw it, from the shackles of the League of Nations, and having already flouted with relative impunity the non-aggression treaties signed by his more liberal countrymen, Konoe had openly been calling for Japan to ape the aggressive expansionist policies of sympathetic states in Europe. 'Italian officials preach with great boldness and frankness why Italy must expand,' said Konoe in a speech in November 1935. 'German politicians openly proclaim in the Nazi program why Germany requires new territory. Only Japan lacks this frankness.'[4]

One month after Konoe's appointment, war broke out in China in the wake of the Marco Polo bridge incident. The full force of modern Western technology was unleashed by Japan on the Chinese population. Towns and cities were indiscriminately bombed, and countless women and children died. The photographs of the carnage caused by the bombs and shells that fell on Shanghai railway station became iconic representations of the cruelty of the Japanese. In September 1937, in the wake of the Shanghai bombing, the American government condemned the Japanese action (in a statement that now has a hypocritical ring to it, given that eight years later the Americans were to bomb Japan on a far greater scale): 'The American government holds the view that any general bombing of an extensive area, wherein there resides a large population engaged in peaceable pursuits, is unwarranted and contrary to principles of law and humanity.'[5]

The Japanese antagonized the Americans still further when, three months later during the attack on Nanking, over-excited pilots sank the US gunboat *Panay* and three American tankers that lay on a nearby river. Two American sailors died in the attack. The Japanese government and military were uncharacteristically quick to apologise for the incident – conscious, no doubt, of Japan's continued dependence on American oil. But there was to be no apology to the world for the war crimes that the Imperial Army committed in Nanking. Britain and the USA, angry at Japan's actions, discussed amongst themselves what should be their best response. Furious at the sinking of the USS *Panay*, Roosevelt even contemplated a naval blockade of Japan using American and British warships. But the plan was never put into effect – the British were not prepared to antagonize the Japanese to that extent.

Whilst at a high political level the Western democracies did little to prevent Japanese aggression in China, Western public opinion was certainly changed by knowledge of what became popularly known as the 'Rape of Nanking'. In one of the first examples of film reporting influencing world opinion, newsreels brought pictures of the suffering inside Nanking to cinema screens all over Britain and America. A typical scene from one newsreel shows a weeping father hugging the corpse of his young child while the commentary intones, 'That man carries the body of his child, clinging dumbly to the forlorn hope that life still inhabits its shattered little body.' Not surprisingly, this emotional reporting had an enormous impact on the sensibilities of the audience. 'We found the Japanese doing things in the world that we didn't think were correct,' says Gene La Rocque, then a student at the University of Illinois. 'For one, the Japanese were raping Nanking, and that was shown in a dramatic way on the movie screen.' All of this confirmed the prejudices about the Japanese held by Americans like La Rocque: 'The Japanese kind of looked like monkeys to us. They were not a very friendly, but also not a very intelligent group of people. In Illinois, where I grew up, in the mid-West of the United States, the Japanese were looked down upon. First of all they were of smaller stature. They were not as big as we were and they looked very funny in caricature. Our concept of the Japanese prior to Pearl Harbor was that they were a weak, not very sophisticated people – so foreign to us. After all, the head of the country was supposed to have been a descendant of God and we thought how primitive that situation was.... We were racist, of course we were racist, but that again comes from the fact that they didn't want to become part of our community in any way. They were foreigners to us, a culture we didn't understand, a language we couldn't understand. They were inscrutable.'

The prevalence of racist views such as these was to have a major impact on how Western nations chose to deal with Japan during the 1930s, and would later influence the way the war itself was conducted. It is often hard for people born long after the war fully to grasp just how pervasive these kind of racist ideas were in the Western world. But in the 1930s there were still men and women alive in the United States who had participated in the brutal, virtually genocidal wars against the Native Americans. Less than sixty years before, in 1879, the state constitution of California had withheld the vote from 'all natives of China, idiots, and insane persons'[6] and racism against black Americans was still endemic. Racism was not merely the prejudice of the uneducated, it was official and – as the Nazis were attempting to prove – scientific. (It is instructive to note that, such was Hitler's racism, he never fully explored the potential of the alliance with Japan. He did not consider it a partnership of equals, though he fully understood its political necessity. His preferred ideal was always a partnership with the British – fellow Aryans – rather than the Japanese.)

The British took their racial beliefs one stage further, with many believing not just that the Japanese were inferior to them, but that they themselves were inherently better than anyone else in the world. 'The British had an inborn feeling of superiority,' says Anthony Hewitt, who was a British officer serving in Hong Kong in the 1930s. 'It didn't matter where you came from, whether you were a dustman or you were a lord, you still thought you were superior to any other nation. A great deal of this was because of the strength and power of the British Empire and because we considered that we were superior to people like the Japanese or the Chinese.' Despite the fact that the British colony of Hong Kong was within sight of the Japanese in China, many British soldiers believed that the Imperial Army did not represent much of a threat. 'The British were superior to everyone and it was ridiculous for anyone to say that the Japanese were so good – some little nation like Japan couldn't possibly be better,' says Anthony Hewitt speaking of the prevailing feeling at the time. 'When they were told that the Japanese Zero fighter was a far better aircraft than the Spitfire, people laughed. They said, "Oh, no, of course that couldn't be true." I think they thought that they [the Japanese] loved flowers and they liked geisha girls all dressed up in lovely clothes prancing around. They were really a sort of fragile race in some ways.'

The view that the Japanese were both 'different' and 'inferior' appears to have been rife amongst the British at the time. In 1935 the

British naval attache in Tokyo wrote a report claiming that his research had shown that the Japanese had 'peculiarly slow brains' as a result of the 'strain put on the child's brain in learning some 6000 Chinese characters before any real education can start.'[7] The commander-in-chief of British forces in the Far East, Air Chief Marshal Sir Robert Brooke-Popham, was similarly prejudiced. 'I had a good close up, across the barbed wire,' he wrote in a letter to the Chief of the Imperial Defence Staff in 1940, 'of various sub-human specimens dressed in dirty grey uniform, which I was informed were Japanese soldiers. If these represent the average of the Japanese army, the problems of their food and accommodation would be simple, but I cannot believe they would form an intelligent fighting force.'[8] On a visit to Hong Kong, Brooke-Popham was just as frank in the views he expressed to Anthony Hewitt and his comrades: 'Sir Robert Brooke-Popham told us that the Japanese couldn't fly at night time because they couldn't see at night and that they couldn't fire machine guns because they were very bad shots. Everything you can think of – all silly little things! Remarks which were totally untrue.'

Hewitt knew that Brooke-Popham was speaking nonsense, because he had first-hand knowledge of the seriousness of the threat from the Japanese. He had seen with his own eyes, standing on the border between Hong Kong and China, just how ruthless the Japanese could be. 'We watched the fighting down below and to my horror I saw them [Japanese soldiers] forming up Chinese soldiers and gunning them to death, which was a horrible thing. It was sickening what went on. But we stood there on that horrible line and saw almost daily some really beastly thing, like a poor Chinese person being robbed and then beaten by rifle butts or even tortured, and sometimes, for no apparent reason, actually shot dead. Straightaway we thought they were very brutal. The mere fact they shot those prisoners made us think that that was what they'd do to us if they attacked.'

In 1937 Hewitt gained further insight into the Japanese when he become one of the few British officers ever to visit their country. He was amazed at the difference between the Japan of British prejudice and the Japan of reality. 'I was astonished to travel on the Japanese railway line from Kyoto to Tokyo. You went in a most super train which went very fast and which was frightfully well built and very comfortable and excellently done. The hotels were marvellous too. I stayed in the Tokyo [Imperial] Hotel and it was lovely – one of the best in the world, I think. It was an advanced country. They weren't like the poor Chinese – it wasn't a third-rate country at all.' And Hewitt's admiration extended to his assessment of the capabilities of the Imperial Army. 'I saw a Japanese force carrying out an exercise and I realized that, from a military point of view, they were very advanced as well. They had excellent weapons, their soldiers were very highly trained, and they were really outstanding.' On his return to Hong Kong he submitted a report to his superiors outlining the extent of the threat he thought the Japanese posed, only to be told that he was 'probably exaggerating the problem'.

As the 1930s came to an end, Japanese foreign policy shifted even further towards the inevitability of a formal alliance with Nazi Germany. In a speech on 20 February 1938 Hitler lauded Japan for attempting to stem the tide of the worldwide communist threat and announced that soon Germany would formally recognize the Japanese puppet state of Manchukuo. But by now the eyes of European states like Britain and France were more focused on the German threat than on the distant Japanese one. Pursuing a policy of appeasement, the British government acquiesced as the Germans first seized Austria and then, in an event that precipitated the Munich conference of September 1938, threatened to annexe the Sudetenland (the German-speaking regions of Czechoslovakia). The Japanese looked on in wonder as the Western democracies appeared to buckle in the face of German aggression. Indeed, there are Japanese who still today look at the desire of the Western Allies to reach a compromise agreement with the Nazis, contrast it with the comparative intransigence of Britain and the USA towards Japan during the same period, and see in this distinction another example of racial discrimination. But the cases are not analogous. Much of the British and American political elite believed that the Versailles Treaty negotiated at the end of the First World War had been too harsh on Germany – particularly in terms of territory, given that so much former German land had been redistributed to countries like Czechoslovakia and Poland. The argument that the German aggression of the late 1930s was merely an attempt to 'right the wrongs of Versailles' was persuasive to many. Opinion polls in the United States demonstrated that the general public were much more prepared to stand up to Japanese aggression in China than they were to German aggression in Europe.[9] The Germans, it appeared, had some justification, however tenuous, for their action, but the Japanese were perceived to be acting out of a straightforward and wholly reprehensible desire to expand their empire.

In the summer of 1939, as Hitler plotted to annexe portions of Poland, the Japanese skirmished with Soviet forces on the Mongolian border. Ever since the Imperial Army had occupied Manchuria there had been tension between the two nations, with the position of the border always in dispute. The fierceness of the Soviet resistance to these border incursions by the Imperial Army, and Stalin's disinclination to find a diplomatic solution to the problem, were at first sight surprising to the Japanese, since the Soviet leader faced a huge threat on his Western border. After all, in his autobiography *Mein Kampf*, published in the 1920s, Hitler had explicitly written of his desire for Germany to expand into Russia in search of *Lebensraum*. But now the Soviet leader decided that it was better to reach an accommodation with his ideological enemy in Europe than to appease the Japanese in Asia. As a consequence, August 1939 was a devastating month for the Japanese. On the 20th, the Red Army went on the offensive on the borders of Manchuria and began to beat back the Japanese. Three days later came the announcement that shocked the world – the Soviet–German Non-aggression Pact. Hitler astounded the Japanese government by reaching an agreement with Stalin that professed to guarantee that neither country would attack the other. It made nonsense of the Anti-Comintern Pact to which the Japanese had put their name just three years before.

In response, on 28 August prime minister Hiranuma, who had replaced Konoe in January 1939, resigned as a result of these 'inexplicable new conditions'.[10] The new prime minister, General Nobuyuki Abe, sought to rebuild Japanese foreign policy from the debris left in the wake of the Soviet–German Non-aggression Pact. With the US government hardening its position over Japanese aggression in China, the new cabinet believed that even stronger links with Germany represented the only way forward for Japanese foreign policy. Hitler was clearly the one international leader who was successfully dictating his demands to the world. His army had swept first through Poland and then, in the spring of 1940, through France. 'When World War II started in 1939,' says Masatake Okumiya, then of the Japanese Imperial Navy, 'Germany's swift growth in power impressed not only the political leaders of the Japanese government but also the military ones. They believed that the Germans would win this war. This belief was the foundation for the Japanese thinking at the time.' The Japanese also realized that, with the German occupation of Europe, colonies like the Dutch East Indies and French Indochina were ripe for the picking. If a formal treaty could not swiftly be made with Nazi Germany, there was a risk that these colonies would be seized by the Germans instead of the Japanese. Thus it was hardly surprising that the Japanese government hurriedly concluded a formal alliance with Germany and Italy, and the Tripartite Pact was signed on 27 September 1940. By now a hard-line triumvirate were shaping Japan's foreign policy: the hawkish Prince Konoe was prime minister once more, the foreign minister was Yosuke Matsuoka, who had spent years on the west coast of America and experienced at first hand the racist views of Americans towards the Japanese; and the minister of war was the belligerent General Hideki Tojo, one of the architects of the Japanese war in China.

On 22 September, just days before the treaty of alliance was formally signed with Germany and Italy, the Japanese took advantage of their friendship with the Nazis by moving their troops into northern Indochina (today's Vietnam). The United States, which had already threatened the Japanese government that it would cut off oil supplies if the aggression in Asia did not cease, now announced that iron and steel scrap would no longer be exported to Japan. But the Japanese ignored the American threat. An editorial in the newspaper *Mainichi Shimbun* proclaimed: 'The time has at last arrived when Japan's aspiration and efforts to establish East Asia for East Asiatics, free from the Anglo-Saxon yoke, coincides exactly with the German–Italian aspiration to build a New Order in Europe and to seek a future appropriate to their strength by liberating themselves from Anglo-Saxon clutches.'[11]

The Japanese then followed the Nazi example and concluded a neutrality agreement with their ideological enemy – the communists of the Soviet Union. In March 1941 foreign minister Matsuoka visited Moscow and reached an agreement with Stalin that guaranteed neither country would attack the other. 'We are both Asiatic,' said Stalin after the treaty was signed, 'now Japan can move south.'[12]

Four months later the Soviet Union was under attack from the other nation with which it had recently signed a non-aggression treaty – Nazi Germany. Hitler once again dictated events when he launched Operation Barbarossa, his gigantic Blitzkrieg assault on Soviet territory, on 22 June 1941. Once more the Japanese gazed in wonder at the actions of the German dictator. There seemed little doubt to the Japanese elite that the Germans would soon conquer the Soviet Union just as they had crushed mainland Europe. And the Japanese were not alone in thinking Stalin's regime was doomed. 'The best opinion I can get', wrote the US secretary of the navy to President Roosevelt on 23 June, 'is that it will take anywhere from six weeks to two months for Hitler to clean up on Russia.' Hugh Dalton, the British Labour politician, recorded in his diary on 22 June: 'I am mentally preparing myself for the headlong collapse of the Red Army and Air Force.' The British War Office told the BBC that it should not give out the impression that Russian armed resistance would last more than six weeks.[13]

The impact on the Japanese of the news of the German invasion of the Soviet Union can scarcely be overestimated. At a stroke the political map of the world was changed as Hitler demonstrated once more how boldness on a grand scale could change a country's fortunes. One immediate consequence was that the Japanese no longer faced any threat from the Soviet Union. Equally, the Japanese noted that Germany – short of raw materials and forced until that moment passively to buy oil and steel from the Soviet Union – had moved in one dramatic moment to snatch and steal what it required instead. What could be a clearer example of a possible way forward for Japan than this?

On 2 July 1941 the Japanese government, against the background of phenomenal early German gains in the Soviet Union, formally adopted the policy of creating a 'Greater East Asia Co-Prosperity Sphere', and, as a first step, decided that the Imperial Army should occupy all of French Indochina. The Americans, having broken Japanese diplomatic codes, were able to read messages sent between Tokyo and the Japanese embassy in Washington, and responded swiftly to this new act of Japanese aggression. On 25 July the Americans announced that all Japanese assets in the USA would be frozen and that there would be an embargo on oil shipments to Japan. Days later the British and Dutch followed the American lead and declared similar sanctions against the Japanese.

The Japanese government now faced a profound dilemma. As they saw it the price of getting the oil ban removed was too high for any truly 'honourable' Japanese to accept – the Americans were demanding that Japan give up hard-won territory in Asia and abandon the cherished ideal of a 'New Order' based on Japanese supremacy. But in order to find new supplies of oil and free themselves from this dependence on the United States, the Japanese Imperial Navy would have to venture out and conquer the Dutch East Indies and *en route* there was the risk of encountering ships of the powerful American Pacific fleet. Admiral Yamamoto, the most brilliant strategist in the Imperial Navy, believed there was one possible solution to the problem. The course of action he advocated was risky, but simple – strike hard against the American Pacific fleet at its base in Hawaii in a daring surprise attack, and then propose a compromise peace that would leave Japan a free hand in Asia.

An Imperial Conference was held on 6 September 1941 in Tokyo to discuss the best way forward. Hirohito was clearly anxious about the consequences of any proposed war with the USA. As he reminded his minister of war at the meeting, he had been promised that the war in China which had begun with the Marco Polo bridge incident in 1937 would be finished within a month – and now four years had passed. How long would any war against America last, he demanded to know.

'Three months,' General Sugiyama replied.[14] The meeting broke up with agreement that discussions with the US government should be continued, but that if an acceptable agreement could not be reached Japan must be prepared to go to war. Hirohito ended the conference by reading a poem composed by his grandfather, the mighty Emperor Meiji:

> All the seas in every quarter
> Are as brothers to one another
> Why, then do the winds and waves of strife
> Rage so turbulently throughout the world? [15]

Just what Hirohito meant by this poem has since been hotly debated, with many believing he was expressing his displeasure at the proposed conflict with America. Others point to it as a defining moment which demonstrates Hirohito's lack of moral courage in not commanding that war be avoided at all costs. But there is another way of seeing his decision to read the poem, one that casts his actions not as those of an ineffectual ruler, but as those of a cynically effective one. Hirohito knew that Japan was backed into a corner. No matter which course of action his government took, there was both potential damage to Japan and potential gain. Hirohito had already demonstrated that he lacked all moral scruple by the way he acquiesced in his army's brutal actions in China, and he was clearly of the view that his generals could seize whatever territory in Asia they liked – but only so long as the Imperial Army did not become overstretched. In effect the emperor had only one demand – that his armed forces succeed in whatever course of action they planned. The poem he read is less a wistful hope that war and conflict be eliminated from the world, and more an expression of his continuing belief that his imperial forces should not enter wars they were not going to win.

The two nations thus entered the last few months of peace unforgiving and intransigent on both sides. The Americans now declined prime minister Konoe's request for a face-to-face meeting with President

Roosevelt, believing from the intelligence gained from breaking the Japanese diplomatic code that there was little chance that Japan would make real concessions. On 16 October, Konoe resigned once more as prime minister and was replaced by the minister of war, General Tojo. Fruitless negotiations began in Washington between US secretary of state Hull and ambassador Kichisaburo Nomura. The Americans still insisted that the Japanese must relinquish gains made in China – an impossibility for the emperor and his Imperial Army. For the Americans, major Japanese concessions over China were an essential part of protecting what had become known to the Japanese as the ABCD encirclement (America, Britain, China and the Dutch).

As November 1941 began the Japanese government realized that they were moving inexorably towards war, and were torn between excitement at finally trying to resolve their complex dilemma by force and the knowledge that they were a small country about to provoke the most powerful nation on earth. With hindsight the subsequent Japanese decision to bomb Pearl Harbor seems almost an act of insanity. But at the time the Japanese government made certain assumptions about how events outside their control were likely to develop, and these assumptions, they thought, made the attack seem a pragmatic, rather than a foolhardy, act. The Germans were at the gates of Moscow and it still seemed likely that Hitler would win against Stalin – and even if he did not win immediately, the Red Army would clearly be held on the western borders of the Soviet Union for the foreseeable future. As for the United States, the argument was less about suddenly going to war against the Americans than about converting into an armed conflict the economic war that had effectively already been declared. There was no guarantee (unless the Japanese capitulated and abandoned all of the imperial ambitions that had driven their foreign policy aspirations for the last ten years) that the Americans would not in a matter of months move militarily against Japan themselves, especially if the Imperial Navy ventured out into the Pacific.

Of course, a major part of the reason, with hindsight, that the Japanese attack on Pearl Harbor seems so reckless in terms of scale and resources is that Japan could never hope to defeat the United States. But that was fully recognized at the time. Admiral Yamamoto, the architect of the attack, always maintained that Japan could not hope to win a long drawn-out war. Equally, the Japanese leadership realized that the notion of the Imperial Army marching through the streets of Washington after a successful invasion of mainland America was nonsensical. The entire basis of the Japanese plan rested on the assumption that the Americans would soon grow tired of the war and want to make a compromise peace. Given what actually happened – that the bombing of Pearl Harbor created in the Americans a powerful desire for revenge against the Japanese – that assumption seems impossibly naïve. But in more recent history there has been at least one clear example of a small country in Asia taking on the might of the Americans and winning just such a negotiated peace – Vietnam. The Japanese notion that the Americans would eventually find a conflict thousands of miles away across the Pacific wearisome enough to want to find an honourable way out of it was not, therefore, inherently a ludicrous strategy. 'America is a big country and we knew that we wouldn't be able to win against them once the war was prolonged,' says Masatake Okumiya, who was in the Imperial Navy as the Pearl Harbor operation was launched. 'But at the time the fleet was the mainstay of military power, be it American, British or Japanese. The fleet represented a nation's military power. So if you destroyed the fleet the damage would be huge. It would ruin President Roosevelt's reputation as a commander-in-chief and he might then be put in a difficult situation.'

So on 7 December, the Imperial Navy attacked the American battleships at their naval base at Pearl Harbor on the American islands of Hawaii, having sailed two-thirds of the way across the Pacific. 'We were so surprised, amazed!' says Gene La Roque, then an officer aboard the USS *MacDonough*. 'I personally thought that it was the United States Army Air Corps who'd mistakenly dropped their bombs on us, until we saw the red circles on the Japanese planes as they flew over.' La Roque and his shipmates were particularly astonished because 'there was nothing about the Japanese that we knew, even on the briefings from our intelligence people, that would cause us to be concerned about the capability of the Japanese. We hadn't seen any of their armaments, their warships — we didn't think they could make good aeroplanes. We thought the Japanese couldn't see well, particularly at night, because in all the pictures we'd seen of Japanese over the years they were wearing thick horn-rimmed glasses.'

If initially the American sailors at Pearl Harbor were dumbfounded by the Japanese attack, their emotions quickly changed. 'We thought, this is a dirty trick,' says La Roque. 'Those stinkers, they attacked us by surprise in our own base, they weren't fair, they weren't honest, they didn't do battle with us at sea — those sneaky Japanese outsmarted us. After all, it was Sunday morning. Many people had gone, or were preparing to go, to church services, and that was another thing that angered us about the Japanese — they attacked us during our church services. We thought they would have better sense than to do that. It wasn't fair.' The 'unfairness' of the Japanese attack on Pearl Harbor was to become a major theme constantly voiced by Americans throughout the war — from the characterization by President Roosevelt in his speech following Pearl Harbor that this was a 'day of infamy' to the US marine rallying cry: 'Remember Pearl Harbor! Keep 'em dying!'

Much of the subsequent historical debate about the attack has focused on the fact that the Japanese did not deliver their declaration of war to the Americans until their planes had already begun their bombing runs at Pearl Harbor — something the Japanese say was a 'mistake' made by their embassy in Washington. But arguably it would have made no difference to American anger even if the declaration of war had arrived minutes before the Pearl Harbor attack rather than hours later. The whole Japanese war-plan had been predicated on the assumption that the imperial forces would catch the Americans completely by surprise. In acting this way the Japanese military were following an ancient tradition last seen in modern times in 1904, when Admiral Togo had led the Japanese fleet in a surprise attack on the Russians at Port Arthur. Indeed, it is hard not to see in the belligerent reaction of the Americans to the manner of the Pearl Harbor attack an attempt to conceal their own shame-facedness at being so complacent and ill-prepared.

If Pearl Harbor was a shock to the Americans, it was by no means an unqualified success for the Japanese. Whilst many of the US battleships were damaged or sunk, the aircraft carriers completely escaped damage since they were at sea on exercise. The carriers had been the key Japanese target – the battleships posed little military threat because they did not have the speed to accompany a carrier task force. As a result, the Japanese attack merely eliminated warships best suited to action in the last war rather than in the coming one. Had the Japanese managed to destroy the land base at Pearl Harbor that might have been a serious blow to the Americans, but Admiral Nagumo, commander of the Japanese task force, broke off the attack early, fearful of the return of the missing carriers.

At Pearl Harbor the Japanese did not destroy the American Pacific fleet as they hoped, nor did they break President Roosevelt's reputation and lay the ground for a compromise peace. Equally, contrary to Japanese expectation, the skill with which the Imperial Navy had conducted the raid on Pearl Harbor did not make Americans like Gene La Roque respect their adversary more – it had quite the reverse effect and confirmed the American prejudice that the Japanese were not just 'sneaky' but scarcely human: 'One has to keep in mind, I do believe, that we had been taught that the Japanese were subhuman when we got into the attack. Of course we had no love for Hitler or the Nazis, but we also had many people in America who were of German descent or of Italian descent. It was an entirely different view we had of the Italians and the Germans than we had of the Japanese. We knew the Japanese were sort of subhuman. We thought they were.'

Just five hours after they began bombing Pearl Harbor, the Japanese attacked the British colony of Hong Kong. Surrounded as the British forces were by the Imperial Navy at sea and the Imperial Army across the border in China it had long been accepted that, as Churchill put it, 'There is not the slightest chance of holding Hong Kong or relieving it.'[16] None the less, the British war cabinet expected the colony to hold out against the Japanese for at least several weeks. But, like the Americans, the British had grossly underestimated Japanese military power.

'First of all we thought they were American planes,' says Connie

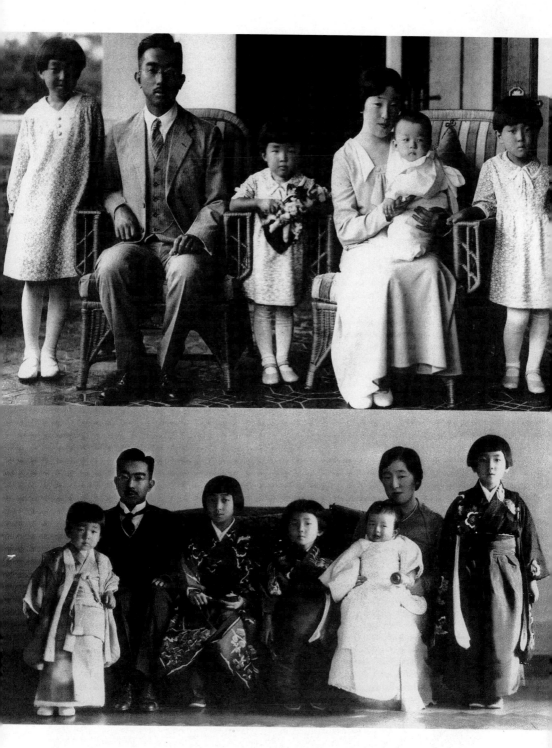

Above The two sides of Emperor Hirohito and the rest of the Japanese royal family: the modern, Western-dressed family group (top) and the family in traditional dress (bottom), harking back to the era before any real Western contact.

Above A formal picture of Emperor Hirohito taken in 1933 when he was 32 years old.
Opposite Militarism ancient and modern: boys in samurai dress (left) and army uniform (right).

Above An early taste of the destruction modern aerial weapons of war would cause. Shanghai railway station after the Japanese had bombed it in 1937.

Opposite top Not the French Riviera but the beaches of Japan – holidaymakers in 1930 when it was still acceptable to partake of Western-style enjoyment.

Opposite below A crowd of 80,000 assemble in Tokyo to celebrate the first anniversary of the signing of the Anti-Comintern Pact in 1937. Four years before Pearl Harbor, the flags of Nazi Germany, Japan and Fascist Italy hang together for all to see.

Above Two scenes of destruction and suffering from the Japanese war against China. No one knows exactly how many civilians the Japanese killed – but at least several million died.
Opposite Two of the sadistic ways in which the Imperial Army dealt with Chinese prisoners: burying them alive (top) and killing them in bayonet practice (bottom).

Above Lieutenant-General Takashi Sakai enters Hong Kong and salutes as the victorious commander less than a month after the attack on Pearl Harbor, which began the war against the Western allies. This moment was, along with the fall of Singapore just weeks later, the high point of Japanese military fortunes.

Sully, then a nurse at the makeshift hospital at Hong Kong's Happy Valley racecourse, as she saw aircraft swoop down from the sky. 'And then, of course, we saw the great sun on them and then we realized.' Just as at Pearl Harbor, those under attack formed the immediate view that their enemy was dishonourable. 'The next thing there were bullets coming out of the wings. We had three Red Crosses on the top of the jockey club, so they could see that – but they never worried about that. Didn't mean anything to them. And I knew from the other places in China they'd also bombed that you couldn't expect any sympathy from them.'

The Japanese eliminated what little hope the colony had of air defence when they destroyed the handful of RAF planes based at Kai Tak airfield before they left the ground. Japanese troops, many from the 38th division and battle-hardened from the conflict in China, made strong early advances towards Hong Kong island after crossing the Sam Chun River into the New Territories.

By 13 December the British forces, outnumbered and with no hope of reinforcement, had withdrawn from the mainland to defend Hong Kong island itself. The Japanese bombarded the island before successfully landing troops on the 18th. Once the Imperial Army had established a firm beach-head they fought their way inland, arriving at the British army medical store at the Silesian mission in the centre of the island on the 19th. Osler Thomas, then a volunteer medical officer with the 4th battery, had spent the night at the mission and had just left to drive back to his unit when he was shot at by the Japanese. He retreated to the mission and from the top windows he and his comrades – a handful of fellow members of the Army Medical Corps – realized that they were both surrounded and outnumbered. 'We were not meant to fight,' says Osler Thomas. 'We were medical personnel, not fighting soldiers.' As a consequence they gave themselves up. 'And it wasn't very long afterwards that the Japanese knocked at the doors and ordered us all out into the courtyard. We went out and the women were separated to one side and the men to the other side. All the men were dressed in khaki, so that there was no distinction between military personnel and civilians. The Japanese then ordered all the men to be stripped from the waist up except for the two of us – officers who were allowed to keep our jackets on.' Of the thirty-three men assembled in the courtyard by the Japanese the majority were civilians; only a handful were army medical orderlies. But these soldiers of the Imperial Army were not concerned about the combatant status of their captives. All the men – civilians as well as soldiers – were ordered to climb the steep steps at the back of the mission until they reached a storm water drain, known by the Indian word *nullah*, which flowed along the side of the hill. Above them on the hillside, looking down at them as they stood alongside the nullah, were jeering Japanese troops who had gathered to watch.

'They made us turn to face the *nullah*,' says Osler Thomas, 'and at that moment somebody broke ranks. I saw a figure jumping over the *nullah* and then run down the hill. There was one solitary shot and he fell. After this happened, pandemonium broke out. And my instinct – I don't know what prompted me – was to fall into the *nullah*. A few seconds later another body fell on to me. As I lay in the *nullah* the water was passing under me and began to get more bloody.' Above him at the side of the *nullah* the Japanese were bayoneting their prisoners – just as they had at Nanking and in countless other places throughout China – and letting the bodies fall forward into the storm drain. 'After about ten minutes everything was quiet. And then I heard somebody walking along the edge of the *nullah*. Apparently he was going around shooting everybody to make sure they were dead and that there were no witnesses. He came over to where I lay. I heard him draw the bolt, I heard him fire the shot, and the body on top of me gave a kick. It was now my turn. Once again I heard the bolt, heard the shot, and the next thing I felt was this severe blow across my face and blood came out of my mouth. I thought that the end had come. I touched my face and it was empty – there was no sensation. There was no sensation in my teeth. Then I thought that my face had been shot away. I knew that my end was coming and I felt absolutely desperate. I felt a sense of hopelessness – absolutely bleak. And at that moment I decided to end my life. The only weapon I had was my pair of glasses. So I took my glasses off, broke one lens and used that glass to cut my wrist. And as I was cutting through the skin I heard someone crawling towards me — it was a British soldier, a corporal, who had a severe gash over his neck where an attempt had been made to behead him with a Japanese sword. I said, "Stay still," and he said, "No, I can't take it any longer, I'm moving." And so he moved further down the *nullah*. I suppose he saved my life, because after that all desire to end my life disappeared.'

Thomas crawled along the storm drain until he reached a series of steps where the water tumbled downhill. Knowing he would be seen if he attempted to escape downstream in daylight, he hid in the stream, shivering and bleeding, until nightfall. When it was dark he made his way down the slippery steps, frightened as he went that he might come across the body of the corporal who had crawled on ahead of him. When he emerged at the bottom of the hill he saw an old woman standing outside a squatter's hut and pleaded with her to give him some clothes. Then, stripped of his bloodstained uniform and dressed as a Chinese, he hid in bombed out buildings until he was able to make his way to a friend's house on the other side of the island. 'Afterwards,' he says, 'you had an intense revulsion for the Japanese — you hated them for a long, long time. We never realized what was going to happen. We thought the Japanese would take over Hong Kong and life would be very much the same — we'd be led away to a prisoner-of-war camp or something like that — but it wasn't so.' Of the thirty-two prisoners the Japanese bayoneted by the storm water drain, Osler Thomas was one of only two who survived.

Whilst Thomas hid from the Japanese after the massacre at the Silesian mission, British troops defended Hong Kong island as best they could: 'We'd had such a blasting of bombing and shelling that I was pretty well battle-happy,' says Anthony Hewitt, an officer with the Middlesex regiment. 'I didn't care what happened. I didn't care whether I was killed or wounded or what would happen, but I just wanted to kill a few Japs. We had a lovely time. We wrote off four Japs who were trying to pull a gun along. Wrote them off. The three of us fired at the same time, and we wrote the whole four off in one burst.' But by Christmas Day the overall military situation had become desperate for the British. That afternoon, Major General Christopher Maltby, the commanding officer of the Hong

Kong garrison, ordered Anthony Hewitt's commanding officer, Colonel Stewart, to stop fighting, make his way to the Japanese field headquarters and surrender. 'He [Stewart] went absolutely white with anger,' recalls Hewitt, 'because he was the last man of all who would ever have surrendered himself. And I got a pole and a white sheet and tied it to it, but he wouldn't let me go with him and he set off alone in the fantastic fury of that battle. Hours later the firing stopped and he came back and he was very distressed. He'd been very badly treated, pushed about and abused, but he'd arranged a halt in the firing and a surrender.'

Even though Hong Kong had been effectively defenceless against the Japanese, no one on the British side had thought that the colony would only hold out eighteen days. Irene Drewery, a child of eight at the time, remembers the incredulity with which her family greeted the news of the surrender: 'A soldier was walking past and shouted up to my mother, "It's over." He didn't say, "It's over, we've won," or "It's over, we've lost." It's just that he said, "It's over." So Mother being Mother, thinking that the Japs would never beat the British, started gathering the servants and all the kids and started walking down the hill towards Stanley. She said, "I can't be bothered to wait for transport to come and take us."' For Irene's mother it was 'unthinkable' that the Japanese could have defeated the British in Hong Kong. Incredibly, she had understood the soldier's remark – "It's over" – to mean that the British had won the battle. 'Before war actually broke out, everyone was going round saying the Japanese wouldn't dare fight us, because they were only little and they were ill equipped and they didn't know how to fight.'

The inability of Irene Drewery's mother to accept the possibility of a Japanese victory was to have tragic consequences for her and her family. 'Probably about halfway down the hill,' says Irene, 'we were confronted by six Japanese soldiers with rifles and fixed bayonets.' They took Irene's mother away and then ordered Irene, her nanny, her twelve-year-old brother and two small girls who were staying with the family to wait in a hut at the side of the road. 'We were sitting in this hut and I started to get really agitated because we'd never been treated like that. I used to go down to the village all the time and the Chinese people there were lovely – we made lots of friends. I got beyond upset, I got angry, and I said to Nanny, "I want to go over and get Mummy," and she said, "You can't go, you've got to stay here, the Japanese won't like it." And I said, "Well, you can't stop me, I'm going to get my mummy." And my brother said, "Well, you're not going to go alone."' Irene, her brother and the two other girls left the hut and started banging on the door of the nearby garage where Mrs Drewery was being held. 'The door opened and they dragged us inside. And when I first went in my mother was sort of half lying up against the wall. She didn't look like my mother looked. My mother was always beautiful and her hair was always well done and her clothes were always neat and she just didn't look like my mum. That's the only way I can explain it – she didn't look neat and tidy any more.' Only years later did Irene understand exactly what had happened to her mother – she had been raped.

As Irene stood looking down at her mother she felt cold steel on the back of her neck: 'I thought to myself he's going to chop my head off. And I just saw this sword go up. I didn't even know if it was a sword – it could have been a bayonet.' At that moment, the Drewerys were the beneficiaries of an extraordinary piece of luck. 'The next thing the door opened, there was a bang and the soldier fell down, and we were being pushed outside. And a man with a Japanese-American accent said, "Stay here!"' A Japanese officer had arrived – a member of the Imperial Army who would not tolerate the rape of women or the murder of children. He went back into the garage where Mrs Drewery had been raped 'and there was a hell of a lot more noise and then he came back outside and said, "Those soldiers will never hurt another living person" or something like that. And he told us he wasn't going to fight women and children and that he'd been in New York and he was called back and sent to fight. Then he stopped a truck that was coming along from the direction of the village and it was driven by one of our soldiers and the Japanese officer asked them to take us back up.'

On the same day as Irene Drewery's ordeal, Christmas Day 1941, Connie Sully too had her first encounter with soldiers of the Imperial Army. At seven o'clock in the morning about fifty Japanese soldiers came down from the hills and burst into the makeshift hospital at the jockey club. 'We felt a bit scared,' says Connie. 'But we'd all been told just to sit down and do things. We made dressings, we rolled bandages, unrolled them, rolled them up again.' One of the Japanese (Connie suspected he was drunk) came in and threatened the twenty or so nurses who sat preparing bandages. After a few terrifying moments the nurses realized that he only wanted one of the nurses to remove her tin hat. 'And when she took it off and threw it away, he just nodded and walked off. The Japanese had arrived so quickly that nobody had a chance to clear the booths upstairs of alcohol. And of course they made their way up there first. And once they got into that there was no stopping them.' When it was dark the Japanese soldiers confronted the nurses once again. 'Someone came and shone their torch round and they went looking round and picked out the youngest.' The soldiers took Connie and two young Chinese upstairs. 'And unfortunately for us, we were all raped. Wasn't very nice. But if you'd tried to do anything you'd have got a bullet. So that was the only way – you had to grin and bear it. I think I valued my life too much to take a bullet. And then when they'd finished they marched us back downstairs again.' To Connie the rape came as the most brutal shock. 'I don't think I'd even had a boyfriend,' she says. 'But we knew what they wanted and we were told "Don't resist" because they don't think twice – they just either stab or shoot you. I didn't really feel anything. I sort of kept my body closed off from anything.' In an extraordinary display of bravery and stoicism, the next morning Connie was back on duty as a nurse: 'We didn't put up a show,' she says. 'It was finished. What could we do? It was the way you were brought up. You didn't run away. That wasn't our upbringing at all. It was just something that happened that you tried to forget, but you never did. Stays with you for ever.'

Appalling as the experience of these British residents of Hong Kong was at the hands of the Japanese, it was, from the first, the Chinese community that suffered most. As Anthony Hewitt was marched through the streets as a prisoner of war he 'saw dead bodies everywhere. I'd watched them, the Japanese, kill people on a cricket ground along the Queens

Road. They were just hitting the Chinese all over the place. Knocking them down with rifle butts, shooting people for no reason, robbing them. It was quite ghastly. I felt terrible. Here we were marching towards imprisonment, and we were the people who were meant to look after the Chinese of Hong Kong and should have defended them, and now we'd left them at the mercy of these ghastly people.'

Demonstrably, the behaviour of the Japanese soldiers who descended upon Hong Kong in December 1941 did not gradually become more brutal as the campaign wore on. As the first-hand testimony demonstrates, from the outset these troops acted in the most appalling way. But the behaviour of the Imperial Army in Hong Kong is explained by conditioning, not by genetics. The soldiers of the Imperial Army's 38th division who invaded Hong Kong had fought in some 400 actions since being posted to south China more than two years before. And the Imperial Army as a whole had been engaged for the previous ten years in a struggle on the Asian mainland against a people who, they were told, were 'below human'. That Japanese soldiers did not exempt Westerners from brutal treatment is, in the circumstances, understandable. Unlike the men of the Imperial Army, German soldiers who fought 'without rules' on the Eastern Front and then relatively chivalrously in the West were able to put thousands of physical miles between their different mental states.

These early days of the Pacific War were days of triumph for the Japanese Imperial Army. The battle plan of the High Command called for a serious of ambitious attacks across seven different time zones – from Pearl Harbor in the east to Burma in the west. And in each of their attacks the Japanese demonstrated a level of military skill that left their opponents reeling. In the Gulf of Siam the Japanese navy sank the pride of the British navy, the battleships HMS *Repulse* and *Prince of Wales* (one deck officer on the *Repulse* had said, on being told the Imperial Navy was nearby, 'Oh, but they're Japanese. There's nothing to worry about' – the next day the Japanese sank his ship).[17] In one air attack on the Philippines, ten hours after the bombing of Pearl Harbor, the Japanese destroyed 103 US planes.[18] In Malaya Japanese forces landed unopposed and moved forward so swiftly as to threaten to encircle thousands of British troops.

But the biggest disaster for the Allies occurred two months into the war when the Japanese, having advanced down the Malayan peninsula, reached the British garrison at Singapore. Nothing illustrates the complacency of the British army more clearly than the fall of Singapore – an event that Churchill described as 'the worst disaster and largest capitulation in British history.'[19] Singapore was an island of vital strategic importance – essential sea lanes lay either side of it – but all the gun emplacements faced out to sea. To the north of Singapore lay jungle that was thought impassable. The only problem was, by February 1942 the Japanese had marched through it. Thirty-five thousand Japanese troops confronted a defending force of twice that number under the command of Lieutenant General Arthur Percival. The Japanese were tough, confident and resourceful. The British and their allies were inexperienced, confused and uncertain. Even though the defenders massively outnumbered the attackers, the British and their allies were spread so thinly around the entire coastline of the island that when the Japanese concentrated their attack on one spot they punched through into the interior. After having been forced back to Singapore town itself, Percival finally surrendered on 15 February and more than 70,000 British and Allied soldiers fell into Japanese hands. In the course of their attack the Japanese had suffered just 3000 casualties. It was their most outstanding victory of the war. Viscount Kido, one of the emperor's closest advisers, recorded that Hirohito was 'very cheerful' when he heard of the fall of Singapore. 'My dear Kido,' the emperor apparently said, 'I know I harp on this all the time, but as I've said before and will say again, it all shows the importance of advance planning. None of this would have been possible without careful preparation.'[20]

In the first three months of the war the Japanese had, much to their own surprise, captured more than 100,000 Allied prisoners. They now faced a profound dilemma – just how should they treat their captives?

PRISONERS OF THE JAPANESE

Appalling as the mistreatment of Westerners in Hong Kong was in the first hours of the war, such cruelty did not represent Japanese policy, but random acts of brutality by individual soldiers and units. Once Japanese authority had been established over the occupied areas there was a search for a systematic approach to the treatment of POWs and civilian internees. In those initial months that policy was influenced by two factors; first, Japan had never ratified the Geneva Convention which laid down humane conditions under which prisoners of war should be treated, and second, the Japanese had never expected to take such huge numbers of POWs so quickly and thus had made little provision for them.

The detailed experience of every POW held by the Japanese is, of course, unique, but the story of what happened to Anthony Hewitt in his first days of captivity in Hong Kong is, in many respects, typical. In common with the vast majority of Allied soldiers taken prisoner by the Japanese, he and his men saw nothing dishonourable in having surrendered. 'I said to them, "You fought wonderfully and you fought with valour, and you have reason to remain proud of that and to retain your pride." And I noticed that they had all shaved and a lot of them had had their hair cut. They'd cleaned their uniforms and they looked incredibly marvellous. And I thought: "They are still men."'

This belief that it was possible to surrender and still retain 'honour' was anathema to the Japanese. Their military code of conduct stated explicitly that no Japanese soldier could ever surrender. Interestingly, the ancient warrior code of Japan had been contradictory on this point – on the one hand the warrior was obliged not to allow himself to be captured but on the other he was supposed to treat those who surrendered to him with kindness. This contradiction meant that when, in the course of conflict on the Asian mainland during the 1890s, General Aritomo Yamagata announced that soldiers of the Imperial Army should commit suicide sooner than surrender, his instruction still did not prevent Japanese soldiers taking enemy prisoners and treating them with relative humanity. But this inherent contradiction always existed and when the Japanese were faced with huge numbers of Allied POWs it was easy for them to extrapolate from this one aspect of their military code – that surrender for the Japanese soldier was dishonourable – the belief that for the enemy to give themselves up in such large numbers meant they were not worthy of respect. This belief that their Western adversaries lacked courage was compounded by the sheer size of the Allied POWs, the vast majority of whom towered over the soldiers of the Imperial Army. 'I think we were all rather shocked and taken aback to see the size of them,' confirms Toyoshige Karashima, one of those charged with guarding Allied POWs. 'We thought: "How on earth are we going to look after people of this size?"'

Moreover, the attitude of these Japanese soldiers to the Westerners they had captured was very different from that of their compatriots who had so generously cared for their prisoners in the First World War. Few in the Imperial Army now wished to be judged by the values of the liberal democracies of the West – Japanese propaganda had, after all, called throughout the 1930s for such decadent thought to be rejected. These Japanese soldiers had been taught that Westerners were interlopers in Asia – what right had these hypocrites (who had so objected to Japan's legitimate territorial expansion in China) to be here at all?

Against this background of Japanese belief, Anthony Hewitt and his fellow soldiers of the Middlesex regiment marched into captivity in Hong Kong and were held at an abandoned barracks at Sham Shui Po. 'The barracks had been knocked about all over the place,' he says. 'The living conditions were quite terrible. A lot of my soldiers were living in huts with no roofs and with nothing to protect them from the rain. They had nothing to sleep on – just bare bits of concrete. There was no medicine and we only got a bowl of rice in the morning and a bowl of rice in the evening. There were flies and rats and everything you can think of in the camp and the smell was ghastly. The sanitation in the camp was out of this world – there was nothing. But the men were still marvellous. The cockney when he's down still keeps his spirit.' From the first it was obvious that the Japanese would treat their captives with great brutality. 'The Japanese were inclined to beat you, particularly if you failed to salute them. This didn't mean facing a Japanese head on and failing to salute him that way, but it might be a Japanese about a hundred yards away that you hadn't noticed.' Hewitt's commanding officer spent 'hours and hours' complaining to the Japanese about conditions in the camp and 'they always said, "Oh yes, that's all right, we'll do that tomorrow, we'll bring in this tomorrow." They never damn well did anything at all. They didn't mean to, either.'

After little more than a month in captivity, Hewitt was told by his commanding officer that he should try to escape from the camp and make his way to China, in order to take letters to the nearest British embassy outlining the terrible conditions under which the soldiers were held. In preparation for his escape Hewitt tried to deceive the Japanese guards about the number of British officers imprisoned in the camp by omitting one sick officer from the roll call – the plan was that the sick officer would then be included to make up the numbers once Hewitt had made his escape. Then disaster struck: 'One unfortunate day he was found and the Japanese came to me and said, "There are more officers than you said." So they took me behind what was the old sergeants' mess and they went on questioning me and then they started beating me. They beat me with frightful blows to the head – mainly with the blades of swords and also with bayonets in their leather folders. I remember thinking about my parents as I was bashed. When I got into trouble like this I always thought of my parents. I was very fond of my father and mother who were in England, and I thought, "Oh God, my poor parents." I would have loved to have seen them again. Very shortly I was unconscious. I was trying not to fall down, because I knew I'd be beaten like mad on the ground but I was completely unconscious and so I must have been beaten as I lay there.' When he came round he was covered in blood and had trouble focusing his eyes – he was to have problems with his eyesight for many years afterwards. But in an act of considerable courage he still managed to escape from the camp in February 1942 and make his way by boat to the Chinese mainland where he joined the resistance against the Japanese. His six weeks of imprisonment had allowed him to form a view of his enemy that would no doubt be echoed by the majority of Allied prisoners who fell into Japanese hands: 'I thought they were terrible people, the Japanese. There was absolutely no link between normal civilized behaviour and the way these Japanese troops were behaving. No reason at all why they had to behave in this awful, cruel and sadistic manner.'

Conditions for both the POWs in the camp at Sham Shui Po and the Western civilians interred in Hong Kong at Stanley camp were grim – all suffered from overcrowding and malnutrition. But even though the Chinese inhabitants of Hong Kong were not automatically interned they too did not escape atrocious mistreatment. Two whole areas, Happy Valley and Wancahi, were designated by the Japanese as enormous brothels, with the Chinese women who lived there forced into prostitution. There was scarcely any food for the Chinese of Hong Kong and, by the end of the war, stories of cannibalism abounded. Some managed to escape to the mainland (where they often fared little better); those who stayed risked death from starvation and disease. By the summer of 1945 the Chinese population of the colony had been reduced from 1,600,000 to 750,000.

This pattern of the mistreatment of POWs and Western civilians in overcrowded camps, together with the oppression of the indigenous population outside of captivity, was repeated across virtually the whole of the burgeoning Japanese empire. Within weeks of their conquest of Hong Kong the Japanese crossed the South China Sea and occupied Java; then part of the Dutch East Indies. 'We thought we were safe, living in the Dutch East Indies,' says Jan Ruff, a Dutch woman then in her late teens. 'Then Singapore fell in February 1942 and we knew it would only be a matter of time before the Japanese landed on Java, which they did on 1 March.' A week later the Dutch surrendered and captured Western civilians were interned in camps. 'It was really dreadful – the starvation,' says Jan. 'You really had hunger pains. We ate anything. We ate weeds. Towards the end we even ate rats and snails. We even ate a cat – the camp commandant's cat – because we were so hungry. And the Japanese were very brutal. The women were beaten and often punished by being made to stand in the sun for hours and hours. Sometimes for punishment we had to bury our food. And all this for small things. If you didn't bow deeply enough, you'd get punished for that.'

Jan Ruff's initial experience in her internment camp mirrored that of thousands of other Western civilians captured by the Japanese and held in camps from Hong Kong to Borneo and Singapore to Burma. Terrible as these conditions were, just as in Hong Kong the indigenous population – especially the Chinese – often suffered worse outside the camps. But Jan Ruff's case is different, and worthy of particular study, because after being imprisoned for two and a half years her situation suddenly changed. 'One day an army truck arrived at the camp with these high-ranking Japanese officers and we thought, "Oh, it's just another inspection again." But this time the order came that all girls from seventeen years old up had to go and line up in the compound – which made us very suspicious. So all the girls lined up and we could see straightaway that something terrible was going to happen. They sort of paced up and down, up and down, looking at our legs and our faces. Then some girls were told they could go back to their mothers and the line became smaller and smaller. They were sort of laughing at each other and lifting our chins and eventually there were ten girls left in the line and I was one of these ten and the fear was absolutely terrible.' The selected young women were told to pack a small case and were then taken to a truck which waited at the camp gate to drive them away. 'We thought perhaps we were going to work in a factory or something,' says Jan. 'But we were suspicious because they wanted the young girls – the mothers especially were very afraid.'

She and the other young women were driven across Java until they reached a large Dutch-colonial house in Semarang, the capital of Middle Java. The house was surrounded by a fence and guarded. Jan Ruff's terrible ordeal was about to begin: 'We were told that we were in this house for the sexual pleasure of the Japanese military. In other words, we found ourselves in a brothel. So it was just as if my whole world collapsed. We protested. But the Japanese said they could do with us what they liked.'

Each of the young Dutch women was given a Japanese name and had her photograph taken and displayed on the veranda of the house. The torment of the 'opening night' of the military brothel is, says Jan, 'engraved in my body for ever.' 'We were supposed to go to our rooms, but we didn't do that. We all gathered around the dining table and we just sat, clinging to each other.' One by one, each of the girls was dragged away. The house was full of Japanese soldiers, laughing and joking. 'I could hear screaming coming from the bedrooms,' says Jan, 'and I hid under the dining room table but of course they soon pulled me out from under there.' She was dragged into a bedroom by a tall, fat Japanese officer who brandished his sword at her. 'He threatened to kill me if I didn't give myself to him. And I sort of made him understand that I didn't mind dying. I said could I say some prayers before he killed me? But then, of course, he had no intention of killing me. I would have been no good to him dead. And he started to undress himself and I realized he would rape me. He threw me on the bed. He tore off all my clothes, and as I lay there naked on the bed he ran his sword over my body, still threatening me with his sword. I could feel the steel. He was just playing with me like a cat with a mouse. And he eventually raped me. The most brutal rape. And it's something you never forget. We were all virgins. We were such an innocent generation. We knew nothing about sex. And it seemed as if it went on for ages. Eventually he left the room and I was in total shock. I went to the bathroom. I just wanted to wash away the dirt and the shame.'

Jan Ruff tried to hide on the veranda after she was raped but she was soon found and dragged back to the bedroom: 'And there was a whole line-up of Japanese waiting and it started all over again. And this went on all night.' At least ten different Japanese soldiers raped her that first night. 'By raping me the Japanese took away everything from me – my self-respect, my dignity, my possessions, my family. I really wonder how I coped. It's amazing how strong you can be. My strong belief in God and my faith and prayer helped me through.'

That first night was only the beginning of many weeks of torment during which Jan and the other girls were repeatedly raped. 'I even cut off my hair,' she says. 'I thought, "I'll make myself look as ugly as possible." I looked absolutely terrible. Didn't make any difference. In fact, it even drew more attention, because everyone wanted the girl who had cut off her hair.' Once a week the Dutch women were subjected to a gynaecological examination by a male Japanese doctor. 'This was just so ghastly,' she says. 'The door and windows were left open and other Japanese military were encouraged to come into the room or to look through the door or window when we were being examined. The humiliation was absolutely terrible. I mean that was as bad as being raped. They humiliated us. We had no dignity left – they stripped me of everything.' When the doctor first arrived Jan pleaded with him to help. 'I thought, "Well, he's a doctor. I'll put in a complaint." I said, "We're here against our will. Surely as a doctor you have compassion, you'll understand?" He just laughed at me. And he ended up raping me. And from then onwards every time that the doctor came for a visit he raped me first.'

After three months of this torment, Jan Ruff and the other young Dutch women were suddenly taken from the brothel: 'For some reason that we never knew we were told to pack our bags and we were transported to another camp in Batavia – today's Jakarta. There we were put in a women's camp, but the Japanese always kept us separate from the other women. They didn't want anyone to find out what had happened to us. And these other women in the camp thought that we had done all this voluntarily. They thought that we had worked in brothels for the Japanese in order to get more food and we were called "whores". That was a terrible thing. And the Japanese told us that if we were to talk about this to anybody they would kill us and kill our family too. So we kept quiet and my silence started there and then – not daring to talk about it.'

Immediately the war was over Jan Ruff broke her silence when a priest visited the camp: 'He gave mass and I was just so happy, so glad. And afterwards I asked if I could see the priest. I just needed to talk. After all I'd been through I thought that he would be a good person to talk to. Before the war broke out I was brought up in Catholic schools and I wanted to become a nun – that was the only life for me, that's what I really wanted. And I said to this priest, "Is it all right if I tell you my wartime experiences?" And I told him what happened to me during the war. And I shall never forget, after I'd spoken to him he said to me, "My dear child, under the circumstances I think you'd better not become a nun." Because one of the things I'd said to him was, "I still want to become a nun – all these things have happened to me but I still want to become a nun." And then I got this answer from the priest. Which made me feel terrible. I felt I had something to be ashamed of. I felt dirty. I felt soiled.'

The only other people she told of her ordeal were her mother, her father, and, after she was married, her husband. 'They're the only three people I told – and for them it was too much. My mother, she couldn't deal with it – her daughter systematically raped by the Japanese military. My father was even worse. And even Tom, my beautiful darling husband, he listened to me carefully but we never talked about it again. It was never discussed. It was just too much. And therefore we had to get on with our lives as if nothing had happened, and it was very hard.'

It was not until 1992 – nearly fifty years after the crime had taken place – that Jan Ruff decided to tell the world of her experience during the war. She was relaxing in the sitting room of her house in Adelaide when she saw an astounding series of interviews on television. Some of the first Korean comfort women to talk openly about the crimes the Japanese army had committed against them were telling their stories: 'And when I saw them on television I thought I must back these women up. They wanted an apology from the Japanese government – they wanted their dignity back. So then I became the first European "comfort woman" to speak out. And when I saw the other comfort women in Tokyo, when I came face to face with the Korean and the Chinese and the Taiwanese and the Philippine comfort women, we threw our arms around each other and we hugged each other, because only we could understand what it was like. Nobody knows – but we did. And when I hugged the other comfort women from Asia it was as if a whole load fell away from my shoulders all of a sudden. We could heal one another. We were the only ones that would understand, because you can never describe it – the feeling. Yes, it was a very healing moment.'

Documents from the Dutch National Archives confirm Jan Ruff's recollections from the war. Altogether thirty-five Dutch women between the ages of sixteen and twenty-six were forced to work in four separate brothels around Semarang in central Java. The first women were installed in the brothels in late February 1944. Three months later, military headquarters in Japan ordered the use of Dutch women as forced prostitutes to cease (though seventeen of them were still sent to a brothel on Flores island where they remained until the end of the war).[1] It remains hard to understand exactly why the decision was taken to put a stop to Western women working in the military brothels in Semarang, especially since from the start of the Japanese occupation of the Dutch East Indies many local Javanese women had been forced into prostitution, but it seems likely that the use of Dutch women in this way was a local initiative. Detestable as the experience of Jan Ruff and the other Dutch women unquestionably was, the suffering they endured was very similar to that of thousands of other Asian comfort women who had been subjected to rape in Japanese military brothels in Asia since the early 1930s.

It is significant that the local initiative to force these Dutch women into military brothels was not taken until the start of 1944, when the war was most definitely going against the Japanese. For Japanese treatment of their captives, whilst not consistent, did often become still more brutal as the war went on – as the history of the Allied prisoners of war held in Sandakan, North Borneo, demonstrates. In the words of Professor Yuki Tanaka, one of the BBC's historical consultants on this project, 'The Sandakan incident provides the clearest picture possible of the relationship between the power structure of the Japanese Army and the occurrence of war crimes.'[2]

The Japanese had been keen to occupy not just the Dutch East Indies but also Borneo (which was divided between the British and the Dutch) because these colonies were a major source of the raw material they needed most of all – oil. To protect this region they decided to use forced labour to build an airfield on the northeast tip of Borneo at a town called Sandakan. The first 1500 prisoners of war – the majority Australian – arrived at Sandakan in July 1942. Initially the death rate in the camp was relatively low. One reason was the availability of morphine, obtained thanks to the subterfuge of Dr Frank Mills, one of the Australian POWs. 'At that time the Japanese were playing the military games to the hilt,' says Dr Mills, 'and they gave the first officer who died a military burial in the town of Sandakan.' After the funeral Dr Mills asked his guard if it was possible to visit the local pharmacy and purchase a dose of morphine for one of the POWs lying sick in the camp. 'He said, "Yes, one dose." I said, "Two doses." He said, "One dose." So we went into the pharmacy and I said in a loud voice, "Give me one dose of morphine sulphate, half an ounce." The little pharmacist took a quick look – a little Indian pharmacist in his early thirties – and took out a packet of morphine and cut it in half and handed it to me. It was half an ounce, about a thousand normal doses. The Jap said, "You pay!" The pharmacist said, "No, too small, no pay." "You pay," he [the Japanese guard] said, "you pay." So I handed over some money and he give me some change and we walked out. I had a thousand doses of morphine. And of course it came in very handy in camp – it was very, very necessary.'

Security was so lax in those early days that around a dozen POWs managed to escape by crawling under the perimeter fence. All of them were eventually recaptured – the area was surrounded by dense jungle and the locals knew that if they were caught helping escaped POWs they would be killed themselves. As a result of these escape attempts the camp commandant, Susumu Hoshijima, acting on orders he had himself received, ordered the prisoners of war to sign a contract pledging that they would not try to escape. Thereafter it was normal practice to shoot any prisoner who escaped, even after he had been recaptured unharmed.

As another security measure the Japanese introduced a special punishment for those prisoners who had committed relatively minor offences – wooden cages. 'They were raised off the ground about two and a half feet,' says Dr Mills. 'The bars were made of wood and they were completely open to the atmosphere. People could only sit in them, not stand. And people went almost out of their mind, at times, in there. It upset the camp terribly. Everyone was on edge, especially when those in the cage were yelling and screaming.' Altogether three wooden cages were eventually in use in the camp. Each day the prisoner would be released for 'exercise' – which consisted of the guards beating him up before locking him back in the cage. Some POWs had to endure 40 days of this torture.

Around the same time, because of the harshness of the work on the aerodrome and the inadequate diet, more POWs started to become sick. 'Beriberi and pellagra were very prevalent,' says Dr Mills. 'Everyone was suffering from them to some degree. The earliest manifestation of this was aching of the feet. People couldn't sleep at night because of their feet aching. They'd walk all night, trudge up and down. It's called "happy feet". People did go to the wall. We did have deaths from vitamin deficiency, and we continued to have them all the time. In general it was a very poor diet, and a lethal diet over a long period.' Jim Millner, another Australian POW, was one of those who complained to Hoshijima about the food, 'and the Japanese commander told us that people die of starvation every day in Japan. You're only POWs – why should we feed you? The Japanese only feed POWs if they work.'

During March and April 1943 another 1200 prisoners of war, the majority British, arrived at Sandakan. Amongst them was RAF officer Peter Lee. He and his men had previously been held in a camp along the coast of Borneo at Jesselton (today's Kota Kinabalu), where they had been imprisoned in an overcrowded local jail and had only been given congealed rice to eat. Initially he thought the open aspects of Sandakan camp an improvement on Jesselton, but it soon became clear that many of the British prisoners, already weakened by two years of imprisonment, would not survive. 'Every day I used to go and see our men in the sick bays,' he says, ' and you'd find a young man that I'd known as a typical example of young British manhood, fit as a fiddle when we were in Singapore. Now you'd either find them horribly emaciated, ghosts of their former self, or incredibly bloated with beriberi, with enormous distended stomachs, their private parts distended, and just lying back naked on the bench. And inevitably, of course, people who'd reached that degree of malnutrition didn't recover.'

Meanwhile, the Japanese were concerned about the lack of progress on the construction of the aerodrome and as a result the brutality with which the POWs were treated began to increase. 'If you didn't obey an order immediately,' says Peter Lee, who worked at Sandakan, 'depending on the personality of the particular Japanese soldier you'd get a crack over the head or a crack over the backside with a stick. There was one occasion when an officer intervened when one of his men was being beaten up, and he was horribly beaten up by quite a number of them. The natural emotion of anyone, any reasonable person, if they're attacked is to defend themselves. But as a prisoner of war of the Japanese you very quickly realized that this was not on. If you attempted to defend yourself you were bashed senseless by the man and his comrades. In this situation you have to take it. In the old British phrase you have to grin and bear it.'

'There was a great deal of bashing at the airport,' says Dr Mills, 'to force the POWs to work harder, and they had a ruthless gang of Japanese who would beat people up. I saw the result of it.' Jim Millner led a work party of Australian POWs at the aerodrome and was 'bashed' by the Japanese 'on many occasions'. 'We had to bow to all the Japanese officers,' he says, 'which was very degrading. And any Japanese, no matter what his rank, could bash you if he felt like it, and they used to take great delight in it. The main thing was to stand on your feet. If they knocked you down, they put the boot in. But eventually, if you stood on your feet, they'd end up with a grudging respect for you and you got away without being too badly bashed.'

However, much to the surprise of the POWs at Sandakan (ignorant as they understandably were of the methods of training used by the Imperial Army), the Japanese guards would, on occasion, 'beat themselves up'. 'To give them justice,' says Dr Mills, 'they did it to themselves. It was their policy. If some soldier was getting down in the dumps or out of sorts he would be beaten up in front of his own group – knocked down, then kicked. Then he would have to present arms to the man who did it. And the incident was finished. It was very good psychologically because they never allowed people to feel sorry for themselves. I have seen funny occasions when the NCO beat up the young

soldier, the lieutenant beat up the NCO, the captain beat up the lieutenant – it went right to the top, beating each other up quite publicly.
We used to applaud it. They took no notice. It was some of the only fun
we got, when the Japs started to beat themselves up.'

Then, in the summer of 1943, the POWs suffered a severe setback.
A resistance group within the camp, led by Captain Lionel Matthews,
had managed, with the help of Malayan collaborators, to build a small
radio in order to listen secretly to BBC news bulletins, whose content
was then passed around the camp. In May 1943 they attempted to obtain
more radio parts in order to build a transmitter – but their luck ran out
and they were betrayed by a Chinese civilian. Immediately Matthews
himself and all the POWs who had been working with him were
arrested by the Kempeitai, the Japanese secret military police.
Originally formed to ensure discipline within the Japanese armed
forces, by the 1930s the Kempeitai were also engaged in political sur-
veillance and their role had become similar to that of the German
Gestapo. The Kempeitai habitually used sadistic methods of interrogation, and Captain Matthews and the rest of the POWs suspected of
being members of his resistance group were all brutally tortured.

Not surprisingly, few former members of the Kempeitai are prepared to talk about their work – which is why the interview we managed to obtain with Yoshio Tshuchiya is so valuable. He joined the secret
police in 1933 when he was twenty-two and remained with them until
1945, by which time he was head of the 'information unit' based in
Qiqihar in Inner Mongolia. He used similar methods of interrogation on
his prisoners to those that his colleagues in Borneo would have used on
the Allied prisoners of war.

Most interrogations would begin by beating the suspect with fists or a
stick, 'but beating exhausts us, so we move on to torture,' says Tshuchiya.
Then the victim might be attacked with a red-hot iron bar: 'The iron bar
was brought in and it was all red with heat and it was hard to stay in the
room because human flesh is burned and it smells bad.' Alternatively the
Kempeitai might use the 'hanging' torture, in which a large stone was tied
to the suspect's body and he was suspended in a position of excruciating

agony for hours at a time. But according to Tshuchiya, who personally tortured at least fifty different people during his career, 'beating or hanging people upside down is not so effective as water torture'. This was his speciality (and it would have been used on Captain Matthews and the other Allied POWs in Sandakan). 'You tie them face up, lying on a long bench,' says Tshuchiya, 'and then you put a cloth on their face and then you pour water onto the cloth so the person can't help drinking it. You push their stomach out with water – blow it right up.' When the stomach was distended the Kempeitai would beat their victim hard on the belly with a stick so that the water was vomited back up. Then they would repeat the procedure again and again. 'During the torture some people are killed,' says Tshuchiya. 'Those people who aren't expert at it kill them, because if water goes into the bronchial tubes and the lungs then they die. You tell by the colour of the face and the colour of the nails. If it's a bloodless face, like a dying face, that's the moment we have to stop. We try not to kill them – but to take them to the verge of being killed.'[3]

The Kempeitai faced the traditional problem encountered by torturers through the ages – false confessions. Since most people will say anything the torturer wants to hear in order to stop the pain, they will often implicate innocent people who in turn are tortured and name still more innocent people. 'Mostly they lied,' says Yoshio Tshuchiya in a frank assessment of the information gained from suspects under torture. But that knowledge didn't stop the Kempeitai trying to obtain what they must have known would be false confessions. 'If we arrested these people and found nothing out, then we would have to carry the responsibility,' he says. 'The Kempeitai would be blamed.' The Kempeitai operating in Borneo during the war similarly did not wish to 'lose face' – and as a result of their torture of the Allied POWs and local people implicated in the plot, thousands of other innocent people were tortured and killed.

The discovery of the resistance group and their radio within the Sandakan camp had one other far-reaching effect. The Japanese, having shot Captain Matthews and the rest of the leaders of the group, decided to separate out the vast majority of the officers in order to deprive the enlisted men of leadership and so make further resistance more difficult. 'At eight o'clock on the morning of this particular day in August 1943,' says Peter Lee, 'we were suddenly informed that we had to be ready – all officers, with the exception of ten who were allowed to stay, had to be ready to move in four hours.' He felt 'great sadness' at being ordered to leave his men: 'It's rather like being separated from your family. I would have given my right arm to have stayed.' Altogether 230 officers were transferred to another POW camp at Kuching.

After the officers left, the 2500 POWs who remained were treated much worse by the Japanese – rations were reduced and even sick prisoners were forced to work. In the autumn of 1944, with the Sandakan airfield nearly completed, more Japanese soldiers were transferred to North Borneo to defend the island in the event of attack. Because of this additional strain on local food supplies, the POWs' rations were reduced still further. The local Japanese commanders also realized that starving the POWs would make them less of a security threat if the Allies landed in the area. A weak and sick POW could not be turned swiftly into an effective soldier to fight the Japanese once again. As a result of this deliberate policy of starving and beating the prisoners, the death rate increased massively and soon a hundred POWs were dying each month – at the start of 1945 only around 1900 remained alive.

By January 1945 bombing by the Allies had made the Sandakan aerodrome unusable. Since the POWs were no longer useful as forced labourers at the airfield, the Japanese decided to use 500 of the fittest as porters for two battalions who were marching from Sandakan to Api on the west coast of Borneo. The first 90 miles (150 km) of this marathon trek of more than 120 miles (200 km) lay through thick jungle. A second march was begun in May which involved all of the POWs who were thought fit enough to attempt it – around 550 men. The remaining seriously sick 250 POWs remained at Sandakan, on starvation rations.

Conditions on both marches were appalling. The POWs, mostly barefoot, had to traverse jungles and swamps rich in snake-infested undergrowth. 'Maybe one in ten of them was sort of healthy,' says Toyoshige Karashima, a Taiwanese camp guard who accompanied them. (Most of the guards the Japanese employed in Sandakan came from

Taiwan – then one of Japan's colonies.) 'But the food situation was terribly bad and a lot of them were sick. They had malaria and things like that, so they were weak.' Karashima and his comrades were under strict instructions to shoot any POW who could not keep up the required pace: 'We were told that if they fell over, we shouldn't leave them. We had to get rid of them. It was maybe three or five days into the march and there'd been very heavy rain the night before, so the prisoners were cold and shivering and about thirty of them couldn't keep up, so we gathered them up and dealt with them.... The only thing we could do was to get rid of them, because they couldn't keep up. The prisoners were put in a kind of valley and so we shot them from above. If they'd had weapons it would have been different – but it made me think, because I have a conscience. But we were told that we had to follow orders, and if we didn't then we would be killed.'

A few days later he murdered again. One of the Australian prisoners fell exhausted in the jungle. 'For an hour I tried to find ways of taking him with me, but I couldn't,' says Karashima. 'He said he wanted to drink coffee and eat bread, but that was impossible. I did have some bread and I'd eaten about half of it, so I gave him the other half. I thought after he ate it he might be able to walk, but he couldn't. He said, "Please kill me", and when I looked at his legs it was very clear that he wouldn't be able to stand up – he wouldn't be able to walk. And his thighs were very swollen. He knew that he couldn't do anything. And he said he was happy to die, and he gave me a photograph and an address. And he asked me to send the photograph to the address. I think it was a photograph of his family. His mother, his father or girlfriend – something like that. But after the war we had a very hard time so I just threw it away.'

After the Australian POW had finished eating the bread Karashima shot him dead: 'I felt very sorry for him, but I had no choice but to kill him. When people were about to die they just gave up once they knew there was no chance of survival. For us, even if I wanted to help him, there was no way I could, except to help him by killing him.'

After the war Toyoshige Karashima was convicted of murdering Australian prisoners of war and imprisoned for more than ten years. But

even today, when pressed, he still doesn't accept his personal responsibility for the crime: 'I don't feel guilty now about what I've done
because in a war people cannot be normal. We had already learnt what
the Japanese were like when we were trained by the Japanese army at a
training camp in Taiwan. When we joined the Japanese army, we were
told that we were the soldiers of the emperor and all we needed to do
was to obey orders – which were the orders of the emperor. That's what
I was told.'

Of the remaining sick POWs left at Sandakan, seventy-five were
forced to set out on a similar trek across Borneo on 9 June, less than
two weeks after the second march had departed. None of this group
survived more than 30 miles (50 km). As for those left at Sandakan, by
July a hundred of them had died, leaving only fifty still alive. Then the
remaining Japanese were ordered to evacuate Sandakan completely.
Shortly before his own death from malaria, Lieutenant Moritake
ordered the execution of twenty-three of the sickest POWs. According
to the later evidence of Sergeant Murozimi, the remaining twenty-seven
had all died of malnutrition and sickness by 15 August.[4]

Meanwhile none of the forced marches across Borneo had reached
the intended destination by the coast – the original Japanese plan had
been ludicrously ambitious (so much so that several Japanese soldiers
had died on the trek, despite receiving much better rations than the
POWs). The marchers actually stopped at the town of Ranau, less than
100 miles (160 km) from Sandakan. At Ranau the POWs who had survived the appalling ordeal of the march through the jungle – about 190
of them – were immediately ordered to build thatched huts for the
Japanese and then for themselves. Then they were forced to carry heavy
loads on their backs from the centre of Ranau to their embryo POW
camp on the outskirts of the town. Other POWs were set to work lug-
ging barrels of water up a hill from a nearby stream. The prisoners were
given even less to eat than before – less than 4 ounces (100 g) of rice
each day – and, as a consequence, every day more and more of them
died. By 20 July the remainder were too weak to work. On 1 August,
Captain Takakuwa decided that the thirty-three POWs who – by what

must have been miraculous powers of courage and willpower – had somehow survived thus far should be killed. All of them were shot.

When Peter Lee heard what had befallen his comrades his reaction was simple: 'Absolute horror! Because nobody at that time had any idea that such a thing could possibly occur in what is called a civilized world.' Of the 1800 Australian prisoners of war who had been alive at Sandakan camp in 1944 only six, who had managed to escape into the jungle, survived. The rest died either in the camp itself, on the marches, or once their trek was over. Every single one of the 700 British prisoners of war lost his life.

The story of what happened at Sandakan is more than a mere catalogue of horror – it is instructive. Because, unlike the Nazi extermination policy which from the moment of its full implementation in early 1942 was a systematic blueprint for murder, the full extent of the criminal Japanese policy towards Allied POWs only emerged piecemeal. There were, from the first moments of the war, instances of murderous brutality like the bayoneting of the prisoners at the Silesian mission in Hong Kong, but this was not the norm. By far the majority of surrendering Allied soldiers survived to become captives of the Japanese, though from the moment they did become prisoners they were subject to mistreatment. Japan had signed the Geneva Convention on the treatment of prisoners of war in July 1929 but had never ratified it. Early in the war the Allies protested at the Japanese treatment of POWs and in response to this pressure the Japanese government did agree in principle to abide by the terms of the Geneva Convention (with the exception of the provision forbidding the use of POW labour to 'further the war effort'). But as these examples from the Dutch East Indies and Borneo demonstrate, this promise to implement the provisions of the Convention was never enforced. The view of the Japanese military was similar to that of the Soviet High Command, and Stalin in particular. Since their own soldiers were forbidden under any circumstances to become prisoners, what was the point in committing to the humane treatment of the surrendered forces of the enemy? In any case, thought many senior Japanese military officers, to treat enemy POWs according to the Geneva Convention was not just onerous, but was to pander to the standards of the Western democracies at a time when Japan should be forging ahead guided only by her own sense of what was right and proper. It was this logic that led to the infamous abuse of Allied POWs as forced labour on military engineering projects like the Burma railway and the building of the Sandakan airfield.

In addition, the Geneva Convention was also utterly at odds with the whole atmosphere of brutality in which the Imperial Army itself functioned. As the survivors of Sandakan testify, the guards would often brutalize each other. As for the Taiwanese guards, at the bottom of the racial and hierarchical chain in the camp, they were so abused that on at least one occasion a Taiwanese guard at Sandakan committed suicide sooner than endure mistreatment any longer.

Once the Japanese had embarked on a policy of treating their prisoners as dishonourable, of working them like beasts of burden and denying them adequate food, clothing and accommodation, a crime like Sandakan was always possible. At Sandakan, only six out of 2500 POWs survived, but this was an unusually high death rate. Overall, roughly 27 per cent of the 350,000 Allied POWs taken by the Japanese died in captivity. In contrast, only 4 per cent of the Allied POWs held by the Germans or Italians perished.[5] There are those who use such statistics to fuel the argument that the Japanese possess some kind of unique 'oriental' cruelty. But that is not the case.

What is less well known is the death rate of Soviet prisoners held in German camps on the Eastern Front during the Second World War. Of the 5.7 million Soviet soldiers taken prisoner by the Germans between June 1941 and February 1945 a staggering 3.3 million died – a death rate more than twice as high as that for Allied POWs in Japanese hands. Moreover, this horrific level of mortality was expected and planned for by the Germans before the war against the Soviet Union began. A planning document from the Wehrmacht's central economic agency, dated 2 May 1941 (six weeks before the war against Stalin began), states baldly: 'Tens of millions of men will undoubtedly starve if we take away all we need from the country.'[6]

The pre-condition for the appallingly high death rate of Soviet prisoners in German hands was the Nazi belief that their enemy was 'subhuman' (just as the similar pre-condition for the criminal mistreatment of the Chinese by the Japanese was the view of the Imperial Army that their enemy were 'below bugs'). But that thought was not uppermost in the minds of the Japanese and their allies as they guarded the Western POWs. The crucial pre-condition in this context was both the knowledge beaten into Japanese soldiers that there were no circumstances under which they could surrender, and the lack of respect they now had for Westerners in Asia (though that lack of respect never extended to thinking Allied POWs were 'subhuman'). As soon as it became clear that the war was lost, it was easy for that contempt to turn to hatred — why, thought the individual Japanese fighting man, should the dishonourable soldier who has surrendered survive this war when I must kill myself instead?

An insight into the depths to which the Imperial Army could sink as a result of their inability to surrender, and the further terrible potential consequences for their POWs, is given by the history of the Japanese army in New Guinea. As early as the end of 1943 it was clear that their situation was desperate. They had landed on the north of this huge island in March 1942 when optimism about the early end of the war was at its height. But a mere twenty months later the Japanese invaders faced a desperate situation as the American fleet destroyed most of the convoys that attempted to reach them. As a result of lack of supplies they began to starve. Forbidden to surrender they found one desperate solution to their predicament — cannibalism. The true story of just what happened in New Guinea was not to emerge until the end of the twentieth century. In 1983 one Japanese veteran of the New Guinea campaign, Shoji Ogawa, wrote of how, at the end of 1943 or the beginning of 1944, he and one of his comrades found the mutilated body of a soldier in the jungle. It was clear that a part of the thigh had been chopped off. Shortly afterwards he describes how 'we were called by a group of four or five soldiers who were not in our troop. They had just finished a meal and there were mess tins nearby. They said that they had a large cut of snake meat and invited us to join in.'[7] Shoji and his friend hurried away, with his friend remarking: 'It's very strange. What do you think they were doing? If that had been snake meat they would never have given any to us. Don't you think they were trying to drag us into the crime they had committed?'

But it was not until the 1990s that a Japanese scholar working in Australia, Professor Yuki Tanaka, managed to get the investigations of the Australian army into cannibalism in New Guinea declassified. After he had studied the documents, a fuller picture of just what had occurred emerged. 'The practice of cannibalism was much more widely practised than previously thought,' Professor Tanaka says. 'Before my research it was a common belief that cannibalism was occasionally practised by individual soldiers. However, I found that cannibalism was an organized group activity.' The widespread practice of cannibalism uncovered by Professor Tanaka extended to instances where Japanese forces had eaten their own dead, the local population, Asian POWs held in New Guinea, and the enemy dead – chiefly Australian soldiers who were engaged in a fierce struggle against the Japanese in an attempt to retake the island.

One of the most horrific cases contained in the newly declassified documents is that of Hatam Ali, an Indian soldier fighting in the British army, who had been taken prisoner by the Japanese in early 1942. At his POW camp 'there was no medical treatment and all prisoners who fell ill were immediately killed by the Japanese. Later, due to Allied attacks and activity, the Japs also ran out of rations. At this stage the Japanese started selecting prisoners, and every day one prisoner was taken out and killed and eaten by the Japanese.'[8] As they became still more desperate Hatam Ali records how the Japanese would hack the flesh from the POWs as they were still alive, before throwing them into a ditch. He knew his turn had come when two Japanese soldiers began taking him towards the hut where the cutting of the bodies took place. He was lucky – he managed to run away from his guards and spent the next two weeks wandering in the jungle before coming across Australian soldiers.

Hatam Ali's story is exceptional. In the vast majority of cases it appears that the Japanese ate those who had already died – particularly the bodies of Australian soldiers killed in battle, obviously preferring to consume this flesh rather than that of POWs or Japanese soldiers who had died of some tropical disease. The Australian documents reveal a litany of gruesome cases – dead Allied soldiers might have their thighs cut off, their buttocks stripped, the heart, liver and entrails removed, their genitals severed and so on. That senior Japanese officers were aware of the problem of cannibalism is clear from an order given by Major General Aozu which says that any Japanese soldier who has eaten human flesh is to be sentenced to death but, significantly, excludes from that punishment those who have eaten 'enemy flesh'.⁹

The stories uncovered by Professor Tanaka are horrific, and seemingly justify the stereotypical belief held by many who fought against the Japanese that they were an 'inhuman' enemy whose actions were 'inscrutable'. But the reason the vast majority of Japanese resorted to cannibalism was simple and understandable. As servants of the emperor they had given their word that they would never surrender. Now, as the war went on and they received no supplies whatsoever, they had to eat whatever they could or they would starve. 'The purpose of this group cannibalism was, of course, survival,' says Professor Tanaka. 'Because about 160,000 Japanese forces were sent to New Guinea in 1942, but 93 per cent of the Japanese forces died.' For Professor Tanaka it is clear where the chief blame for these terrible crimes lies: 'I feel angry towards the Japanese officers who made this decision to send such large numbers of Japanese soldiers to New Guinea without sufficient preparation. And when the situation changed they simply decided to abandon those soldiers.' In addition, Professor Tanaka is at pains to contextualize the actions of Japanese soldiers by pointing out the nature of the jungle warfare they faced. Unlike the Australians, who, he says, 'had the luxury every day after the battle of food and coffee, the Japanese never had this sort of psychological luxury. Day after day and night after night they have to feel surrounded by their enemies, not knowing when they would be attacked. And you don't know what will happen to your psyche after thirty or forty days of this.'

Whilst it is true that in the vast majority of cases of cannibalism in New Guinea the Japanese were driven to commit the crime out of sheer hunger, there are a handful of other, still more disturbing, examples where the motivation is less clear. Bill Hedges was a witness to one such case. As a corporal in the Australian army, he was part of the force which fought the Japanese back across the Owen Stanley mountain range after their failed advance towards Port Moresby. 'The Japanese were the most ferocious enemy you could have wished for,' he says, 'because they didn't value their own lives at all.' He led a patrol of forty men into an encounter with the Japanese at Templeson's Crossing; after a fierce fire-fight he and his soldiers were forced to retreat, leaving behind six Australian dead and four wounded. The next day, once reinforcements had arrived, they managed to retake the position and were astonished at what they found. 'The Japanese had cannibalized our wounded and dead soldiers,' says Hedges. 'We found them with meat stripped off their legs and half-cooked meat in the Japanese dishes. And we were very shocked and surprised to think that our enemy was that dirty.' One of his closest comrades had fallen victim to the Japanese in this way. 'I was heartily disgusted and disappointed to see my good friend lying there, with the flesh stripped off his arms and legs, his uniform torn off him. It's one terrible feeling for anyone, that is. He was a happy country boy, same as 90 per cent of the battalion was.' Thus far Bill Hedges' story is typical of those cases of cannibalism that occurred as a result of Japanese hunger. But then came the discovery that fundamentally changes this percep-tion. 'We found dumps with rice and a lot of tinned food. So they weren't starving and having to eat flesh because they were hungry. So it wasn't for the want of tucker at all.'

The certainty that, in a case like the cannibalism of Bill Hedges' com-rades, the Japanese had adequate food supplies when they committed the crime, leads to the disturbing question: why were the Japanese acting in this way? Hedges finds it hard to speculate: 'Some said it gave them more fighting spirit over the enemy and so forth. But I wouldn't know – you'd have to ask someone with more brains than me.' When Professor Tanaka discovered the occasional case of cannibalism committed when the Japanese still appeared to have sufficient supplies, he formed the view that 'this was practised in order to consolidate solidarity amongst mem-bers of the unit. If you break the taboo together then you feel you are part of the crime – part of the ritual. If you do not participate in this group ritual then you'll be ostracized.' In addition, he feels 'it was an act which helped the Japanese soldiers to numb the fear of jungle fighting'.

The notion that the Japanese were eating dead Australians out of group solidarity even though they were not starving is an intriguing one. In China, as seen earlier, soldiers could be put under pressure to take part in group rape in order to be accepted as members of the group. Hierarchy was all. If you failed to follow the lead of those above you – even if that meant you committed a crime – then you faced the worst punishment of all, exclusion from the group.

Professor Tanaka is at pains to point out that cannibalism has occurred in other desperate wartime situations – not least on the Eastern Front, where starving Soviet prisoners resorted to eating flesh from their comrades who had died in the camps. But he admits that he cannot find a parallel in modern history for the situation Bill Hedges encountered, where the desire to escape starvation was not the prime motivation.

However, the context in which the crime was committed does offer an additional clue as to why it occurred. These Japanese soldiers had been fighting in arduous jungle conditions for many months and may have already had to eat human flesh in order to survive – they would almost certainly know that their starving comrades elsewhere had resorted to the crime. Now, even in the presence of basic supplies like rice, they chose to eat the flesh of their enemy in the knowledge that cannibalism was an accepted mode of behaviour within the group. Crucially, these Japanese soldiers knew that their country was losing the war and that they must die rather than surrender – it must have seemed unlikely in the extreme that they would ever be punished for such a crime. The combination of this situation and this knowledge led to these bizarre and criminal circumstances in which Japanese soldiers decided to eat human 'meat' with their rice.

Japan had never lost a war before. The systems, values and beliefs of Japanese society were consequently put under a strain never before experienced. And, as Chapter 4 demonstrates, as the war turned further against them, Japanese behaviour was to become stranger still.

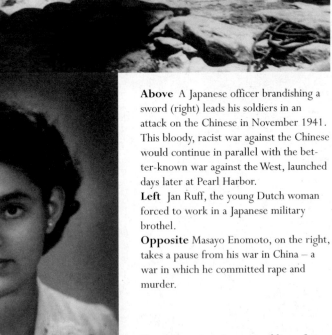

Above A Japanese officer brandishing a sword (right) leads his soldiers in an attack on the Chinese in November 1941. This bloody, racist war against the Chinese would continue in parallel with the better-known war against the West, launched days later at Pearl Harbor.

Left Jan Ruff, the young Dutch woman forced to work in a Japanese military brothel.

Opposite Masayo Enomoto, on the right, takes a pause from his war in China – a war in which he committed rape and murder.

Previous page Japanese soldiers after capturing a Chinese village in the summer of 1938. The world knew of the Rape of Nanking six months before – much less publicized were the atrocities committed by the Imperial Army in the campaign that followed.

Above British soldiers captured after the fall of Singapore in February 1942. Seventy thousand British and Allied soldiers became prisoners of the Japanese in the largest surrender in British military history.
Below Allied prisoners of war en route to a Japanese prison camp.

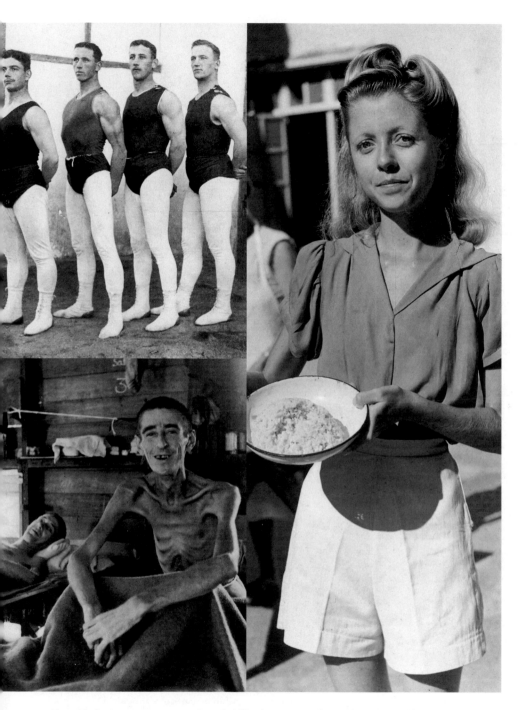

Above left German prisoners of war held by the Japanese during the First World War. These soldiers, humanely treated by their Japanese captors, are dressed for gymnastics.
Below left An Allied soldier after years of captivity during the Second World War.
Right A civilian internee in Stanley Camp, Hong Kong, displays the daily rations for five people, her own emaciated body further proof of the dearth of food in the camp.

Above An allied air reconnaissance picture of Sandakan prisoner of war camp in northern Borneo.
Below The graves of some of the 2500 Allied POWs who perished at Sandakan, either dying on the forced march through the jungle, at the camp itself, or after they finished the trek.
Opposite Bill Hedges (left), a corporal in the Australian Army. He fought the Japanese in New Guinea, and found clear evidence of the cannibalism practised by the Imperial Army.

Above The aftermath of the Japanese attack on the American naval air station at Pearl Harbor on 7 December 1941.
Below More destruction after what Roosevelt called 'the day of infamy' — American warships lie wrecked at Pearl Harbor.

LURCHING
TOWARDS
DEFEAT

The war turned quickly for the Japanese. Just four months into the conflict, the Japanese High Command witnessed disturbing signs that they had fundamentally misjudged the power and resourcefulness of their enemy.

In the early hours of 18 April 1942 Colonel James Doolittle of the United States air force led sixteen B-25 bombers on raids on Tokyo and several other Japanese cities. Launched from an aircraft carrier in the Pacific the planes had to fly over Japan, drop their bombs and then land at airfields in China controlled by the Chinese Nationalists. The bombing was a symbolic morale-boosting gesture by the Americans – and it caused consternation in Japan. How was it possible that their proud capital city, the home of the divine emperor himself, could be subjected to an American air raid? Never in Japanese history had an enemy struck the homeland in such a provocative way. The response of the Japanese government to this humiliation was hugely significant. Eight of the American pilots were captured when their B-25s were shot down over Japanese-controlled regions of China. They were immediately sentenced to be executed because, it was deemed, they had committed a war crime. (The Imperial Army appear not to have appreciated their own double standard in this regard – the Japanese had, of course, been bombing civilians in China for many years.) Even though prime minister Tojo was against the executions at first, he was swayed by the views of his senior military commanders, all of whom wanted the fliers killed. Hirohito stepped in and personally commuted five of the death sentences. Eventually, three of the Americans were executed.

The Doolittle incident is important because it demonstrates both the lack of foresight of the Japanese government (had they never thought Japan might be bombed?) and their misjudged response once they had captured the Americans. The High Command clearly felt that if the B-25 pilots were executed it would deter future raids. Similar thinking had led the Japanese to believe that a sharp defeat at Pearl Harbor would cause the United States to be circumspect in its subsequent dealings with Japan. It was a colossal error of judgement, which revealed the profound ignorance of the High Command about how Western nations were likely to respond to Japanese aggression. Pearl Harbor had sparked the fire of American anger, and the execution of the pilots from the Doolittle raid fanned it still further. (It is also interesting to note that Hirohito was never held to account by the Americans at the end of the war for his decision *not* to commute the death sentences on the three pilots who were executed – it is hard to imagine how a Nazi leader who acted in a similar way would have escaped punishment at the hands of the Allies.)

Just as their reaction to the Doolittle raid demonstrated the political naiveté of the Japanese in thinking that by executing the fliers they would be able to prevent the Americans making further air attacks, so the two great sea battles of summer 1942, first at the Coral Sea and then at Midway, showed how militarily the Japanese had miscalculated the likely turn the war would take. At the battle of the Coral Sea, fought in early May, the Allied fleet sought to prevent the Japanese landing at Port Moresby in New Guinea. This was the first naval battle in history in which the opposing ships never came in sight of each other. It was a reminder to the Japanese – if one was needed – of how disastrous it had been to destroy only the American battleships at Pearl Harbor. For the Pacific War was to be a conflict in which the carriers were king.

Admiral Nimitz, overall commander of the American Pacific fleet, knew of the planned Japanese invasion from intelligence intercepts. As a result two task forces, each based around an aircraft carrier, the USS *Lexington* and the USS *Yorktown*, together with a third force of destroyers and cruisers, moved on the Japanese Imperial Navy under the command of Vice Admiral Shigeyoshi. As battle was joined, the Americans had initial success when their warplanes sank the Japanese carrier *Shoho*. On 8 May, the day of the fiercest conflict, the Americans inflicted damage on another Japanese carrier, the *Shokaku*, but the fighters and bombers of the Imperial Navy fought back successfully, sinking the *Lexington* and severely damaging the *Yorktown*, with the result that the battle was an uneasy draw. The Japanese had succeeded in inflicting more damage on the Americans than they sustained themselves, but their landing at Port Moresby had been prevented. Moreover it was the Americans, with their superior industrial capacity, who were far better equipped to replace their losses.

If the battle of the Coral Sea had been a draw, there was no question about the result of the battle of Midway, fought one month later in early June. It was a decisive American victory, and in many ways the turning point of the war. After a mere six months of success, the Japanese were about to embark on three years of relative failure. Vital to the American success at Midway was, once again, the use that Nimitz made of intercepted intelligence material. He trusted absolutely the information given to him – that the great Admiral Yamamoto, architect of the Pearl Harbor attack, was directing his main thrust against the islands of Midway, US territory far out in the Pacific. That intelligence, combined with false signals information generated by the Americans which led the Japanese to believe that the USS *Hornet* and USS *Enterprise* were not in the area, was to prove decisive. Because he did not believe these carriers were nearby, Vice Admiral Nagumo (surprisingly still in command of an Imperial Navy task force after his less than striking performance at Pearl Harbor) allowed his planes to be caught by surprise on the deck of his own carrier. Four Japanese carriers were eventually sunk at Midway, and Yamamoto was forced to abandon the whole Midway operation.

In Japan the enormous significance of the Midway defeat was not immediately appreciated. In a striking example of how the Japanese High Command structure was flawed and interwoven with rivalries, it took some time for the Imperial Navy even to admit the extent of the defeat to their army colleagues (though they did tell Hirohito their true losses). Viscount Kido, who talked to the emperor about Midway on 8 June

1942, records: 'I had presumed the news of the terrible losses sustained by the naval air force would have caused him untold anxiety, yet when I saw him he was as calm as usual and his countenance showed not the least change.'[1] It is not possible, of course, to know for certain the exact reason Hirohito reacted to the news of Midway in this way, but the evidence of his past behaviour in similar circumstances points to his insouciance being the result of a blissful inability to comprehend that the war had turned, rather than a calculated brave face in front of his subordinates. Just two months later, however, Hirohito and the rest of the Japanese High Command were to become all too aware of the appalling mistake they had made in thinking the Americans would soon tire of the war and sue for a compromise peace.

On 7 August, 19,000 men of the US 1st marine division landed on the island of Guadalcanal in the Solomons group. It was the start of the Allied counter-offensive – something the Japanese had thought could not possibly be mounted so soon. The Americans, in a taste of the horrors to come during their 'island-hopping' campaign, found dislodging the defenders hard and bloody. The Japanese poured reinforcements into the area and for a time the Imperial Navy had supremacy of the sea. US marines, deprived of vital supplies, fought fiercely to defend Henderson Field, the airstrip in the centre of the island. In October Vice Admiral Halsey took command of US naval operations in the area and immediately pursued a more forceful and effective naval strategy. (Halsey's character is best illustrated by his promise after Pearl Harbor that by the end of the conflict 'Japanese would only be spoken in hell.')[2] In September the Japanese managed to come as close as 1000 yards (900 m) to the vital airstrip. But still the marines held out. At sea Halsey's fleet managed to stop Japanese battleships shelling the American positions, and so the planes operating from Henderson Field (the 'Cactus Air Force') were able to destroy many of the Japanese reinforcements as they landed on the beaches.

By the start of 1943 the US position on the island was secure and the Japanese had to pull back to islands in the northern part of the Solomons. Victory had come at a heavy cost – more than 6000

Americans killed or wounded – but it was worth it. Guadalcanal marked the moment at which the Japanese land advance was turned around. With Midway at sea and Guadalcanal on land the Allies had demonstrated that they were more than likely to win this war. The only problem was that despite losing 24,000 men on Guadalcanal the Japanese government showed no signs of wanting to sue for peace. Moreover, the soldiers of the Emperor were fighting with a determination that astounded their opponents.

From the first moments of the war the Americans had noticed a peculiar characteristic of their enemy. 'I remember one incident when we were capturing our first island,' says Gene La Roque. 'We'd appeared to have subdued the few Japanese that were defending the island, and in the late afternoon a couple of my shipmates and I saw this Japanese patrol boat – probably about 150 feet [45 metres] long – and we decided to go over and see how these Japanese lived, because we didn't see anybody on board. As we approached this boat in this lagoon on a peaceful afternoon, two men rushed out from down below, and we thought they were probably going to surrender or that they were going to shoot at us. Instead they went up on the bridge structure, walked out and back and hung themselves right before our eyes from the yardarm. That gave us a good idea of what we were up against. These folks were not gonna give up easily.'

Both on land and at sea the Japanese demonstrated from the first that they were prepared to die sooner than surrender. As already seen, one reason for this devotion to duty is clear – the Imperial Military Service Code instructed members of the armed forces not to 'bring shame' on themselves and their families by becoming prisoners of war. But that is not the whole story – after all, Stalin had issued similar instructions to the Red Army but that had not prevented whole Soviet armies surrendering to the Germans. Crucial to the determination of the Japanese not to give up was the role of the emperor – their belief that their supreme commander was a god played a powerful part in making the Japanese armed forces fight to the end. 'We were told that the emperor was a living god,' says Hajime Kondo, then a soldier in the

Imperial Army. 'If you go to war and die in action then you become a god and are enshrined at the Yasukini shrine and the emperor will kindly come and pray for you.' The consequence of this was clear – 'We never thought of surrender.'

The ferocious way in which the Japanese were prepared to fight to the death did not make the Americans respect them more – it had quite the opposite effect. 'I thought they were very cruel, they were sadistic,' says Michael Witowich of the US Marine Corps, 'and they wanted to die for the emperor, and we had to go out there and help them die for the emperor.' Witowich fought right across the Pacific with the marines. He had first-hand experience of just how fiercely the Japanese were pre-pared to defend every inch of land, sea and coral reef they held. Taking the tiny island of Tarawa in the Gilbert Islands in November 1943 he describes simply as 'Hell'. Rear Admiral Keiji Shibasaki, the commander of the island, had instructed his men to construct a deep series of defence tunnels and pill boxes. He boasted that Tarawa 'could not be taken by a million men in a hundred years.'[3] As a result, the landing was one of the most tortuous the US Marines ever attempted. 'As we were going in the boat got hooked on the coral,' says Witowich, 'because the tide was going out. Two of us went out and then a shell hit the boat. Bodies just blew all over – parts of bodies, heads, legs. And we started swimming waist-deep to the beach. How could you help them [fellow marines] when your job was to go in and fight the Jap? How could you save them in the water?' Once he moved off the beach he attacked the Japanese defences: 'I blew a lot of them out of the caves. We put gasoline in the slits of the pill boxes and lit it with a flame thrower and we shot the hell out of them as they were going out.'

Tarawa did not hold out the 'hundred years' that Keiji had prom-ised, but just three days. Yet it cost 1000 American dead to take the island – with the Japanese losing five times that number. 'You can imag-ine the smell that was there on Tarawa,' says Michael Witowich. 'It's like cat manure. It's horrible. Makes you want to puke. I put some cotton in my nose but the smell was still horrible, with the maggots crawling over the bodies, over their eyes and mouth. And we sat there eating our rations — a dead Jap here, a dead marine there.' After taking part in the fight for Tarawa he became 'very bitter about losing my buddies. Seeing them lying there, burying them, leaves an awful feeling in your heart. Fellas that you trained with, went on liberty with — young kids, sixteen, seventeen.'

Experiences such as these helped fuel in the US marines a deep hatred of the Japanese — a hatred that found one expression in the mutilation of Japanese war dead. Some American marines took the heads of Japanese soldiers, boiled them and kept the skulls as souvenirs. *Time* magazine even carried a photograph during the war of a young woman, the girlfriend of an American sailor, gazing wistfully at a present that her boyfriend had sent back from the Pacific — a Japanese skull signed on the cranium by him and his comrades. Marines also smashed open the corpses' jaws. 'They would turn these bodies over and hit them in the back of the head with the butt of a rifle,' says Paul Montgomery, a US air force pilot who witnessed such atrocities. 'I saw marines that had a paper sack of gold teeth — it weighed probably 10 or 15 pounds [4 or 6 kg]. I saw one marine that had a considerable sack of gold teeth he was gonna take home with him. Now, that's rather brutal.... The marines I met they were just kids — seventeen, eighteen, nineteen years old — and they appeared to me to be a bunch of animals. They told me, "Our chance of getting back to the United States is very slim and we're just going to make the most of it." They were committed, they were determined they were not going home, and they were very mean. They'd be fighting in the chow line, they'd be fighting amongst themselves. Every opportunity they got they'd be in hand-to-hand combat — just because they were on edge.'

It is rare for an American serviceman to confess personally to committing atrocities on war dead — but during our interview with him, Michael Witowich did: 'I shot him [one of the Japanese dead] in the head with a .45 and automatically the mouth opens up. Man! All them gold teeth staring at me. And I didn't knock them out with a rifle, but I used pliers. I had a whole canteen of gold teeth. That's kind of cannibalistic, but during the war everything is horrible. I guess I just had so much hate while I was doing that, you know. There are a lot of atrocities in war — on both sides. Not only on one side, on both sides. Call it revenge, call it what you want.'

'Everyone wanted souvenirs,' says James Eagleton, another former marine. 'I got home with a couple of Japanese rifles and a Japanese flag.' As far as the more ghoulish souvenirs were concerned, he told us that 'in the two years I was overseas I saw one head of a Japanese soldier put on a stick. And our Roman Catholic priest just blew his top, because the lieutenant that had done this was one of his parishioners.'

The atrocities committed by the Japanese during the war are common knowledge, but these atrocities committed by the Americans have received a great deal less publicity. During research for this project it became clear that many US marines had witnessed or participated in mutilation of the Japanese dead, but few wanted to talk about it openly. How common this kind of behaviour was is hard to establish, but anecdotal evidence suggested that it occurred a great deal. When Charles Lindbergh was flying back home to America after visiting the Pacific during the war, he was asked at Hawaii if 'he had any bones in his baggage'. He was informed that this was a 'routine question.'[4]

All of which begs the question: why did American marines treat the Japanese dead in this way? There is no evidence that the mutilation of war dead occurred in any comparable way amongst Allied troops during the conflict in western Europe. But from the start, the conflict in the Pacific was different. Hatred of the Japanese, of course, pervaded everything the marines felt and did. But it was a hatred supported by other emotions – a residual guilt, perhaps, at the way these 'sneaky' Japanese had managed to take them by surprise at Pearl Harbor ('We're gonna have to slap the Dirty Little Jap' go the lyrics of a popular song of the time.) The desperate way in which Japanese soldiers were prepared to fight to the death also contributed to a sense that they were not 'human' in the way that Westerners were, as did the knowledge of the mistreatment of Allied POWs in Japanese hands and the other-worldliness of the Japanese system of government with a god-emperor at its head. There was also simple incomprehension at the propensity of the Japanese to commit suicide rather than be taken alive ('I thought the point of fighting in a war was to try and survive it,' one American serviceman said to us over a cup of coffee after his interview).

At the start of the war the Japanese had been dismissed as 'inferior' warriors, but in the wake of Pearl Harbor and the swift Japanese victories in Southeast Asia that perception had changed to one of grudging acceptance that they were a tougher adversary than had first been believed – but they were still not credited as being 'civilized'. The logic was simple – and perverse: the Japanese were now thought to be formidable opponents precisely because they were prepared to fight in ways that no civilized soldier would be willing to.

It is significant that German soldiers went through a similar process of shifting belief during the campaign on the Eastern Front. Once the Red Army had demonstrated their considerable resilience in cities like Stalingrad, the Germans gained a reluctant respect for their enemy, but it did not make them rethink the propaganda image of the Slavic fighter as 'subhuman'. Just as with the American view of the Japanese, the paradox was that their image of the enemy could change from one of incompetence to super-competence without altering the original bedrock of prejudice and racism.

The Japanese, of course, had entered the war on a not dissimilar platform of prejudice – convinced that the Americans would not have the stomach for a long fight. The Japanese plan for the Pacific War had always been to win a string of quick victories, disable the American fleet, secure the boundaries of the new Japanese empire and then make a compromise peace. No thought had been given to what would happen if the enemy started winning decisive victories, and then showed no inclination to end the war without the unconditional surrender of the Japanese. Given the enormous resources of the United States it was obvious to everyone that a long war would be calamitous for Japan. 'From the time when our line along the Owen Stanley Mountains in New Guinea was broken through [September 1942] I lost hope of victory,' Hirohito recorded in his monologue after the war. 'So I thought that by thrashing the enemy somewhere we would be able to gain a negotiated peace. But we had a treaty with Germany against concluding a separate peace; and we could not violate an international agreement. So I was more or less thinking wouldn't it be good if Germany was quickly defeated.'[5]

The disingenuousness of Hirohito's explanation as to why for three bloody years Japan continued a war he knew could not be won is breathtaking. The notion that he did not want to make peace out of fear of violating an 'international agreement' made with Nazi Germany is nonsensical, given that in the course of the war in China Japan had broken a series of treaties (not least the whole raft of agreements signed at the Washington Conference in the early 1920s). The Nazis, too, had shown their contempt for international agreements when they smashed into the Soviet Union in blatant disregard of the Non-aggression Pact signed in 1939 (Goering once memorably described international treaties as 'so much toilet paper'). A more plausible explanation for Hirohito's position was that he wanted to continue fighting in order to preserve the 'institution of the emperor' and in the process save his own skin. As a result, his strategy of chasing one decisive victory as a stepping stone to suing for a compromise peace — by which he meant a settlement which would leave him on the throne — was to have disastrous consequences for the country he governed.

The next eighteen months brought the imperial forces nothing but a string of defeats throughout their fledgling empire. The first half of 1943 brought the loss of Guadalcanal, the fall of Buna in Papua and defeat in the Aleutian Islands. After a lull in the summer of 1943 the autumn brought more disasters with the successful Allied landing at Finschhafen in Papua, whilst 1944 dawned with the Americans landing on the Marshall Islands. In February that year, in the face of defeat after defeat, prime minister Tojo attempted to consolidate his position and ensure the cooperation between the navy and the army that had previously been lacking by replacing the army chief of staff, Sugiyama, with the only man he felt was up to the job — himself, whilst the chief of the navy staff was replaced by Tojo's creature Shimada. With this new team in place, Tojo believed the Japanese could at last win the decisive victory that would pave the way for peace. The setting for this great victory would be the battle for the island of Saipan in the Marianas and the conflict in the seas around it.

Saipan was not just another in the long line of islands that the Japanese had tried (and failed) to defend for the last two years. Unlike the others, it was territory that had been held by the Japanese before the war. Even though, since the island was held as a mandate, this was not strictly speaking Japanese soil, the arrival of the Americans on its shores marked a worrying development for the Imperial High Command. If the enemy was not exactly at their doorstep, they had certainly arrived in their backyard.

The 2nd and 4th US marine divisions, comprising some 77,000 men, landed on Saipan on 15 June 1944. The geography of the island was ideal for the defenders, with high ground overlooking the landing beaches. The 32,000 Japanese troops under the command of Lieutenant General Yoshitsugu Saito inflicted heavy casualties on the marines beneath them as they came ashore. 'How I ever went through the twenty-five days and twenty-five nights on Saipan, I don't know,' says Michael Witowich, one of the US marines who took part in the battle. 'Day in day out, day in day out, no sleep. Only God would know the suffering you've got to go through. I can't forget my buddies, the horror, seeing them dying and screaming, "Help! Help!" There's nothing you can do. Guys that are screaming and yelling. Horrible. You can see pictures, you can read about them, but you have to be there to listen to the death rattle and the feeling that you get by seeing what's happening. It's horrible.'

As the marines fought on the beaches, Saito was convinced that the approaching Japanese fleet would sink the American ships that were supplying the attackers. But it was not to be. Once again, in the ensuing sea battle the Japanese experienced disaster, losing three aircraft carriers and 500 planes. American reinforcements poured on to the island. Given that it was forbidden for Japanese troops to surrender, Saito could do nothing more than retreat to defensive positions in the centre of the island and fight to the end – and the end came three weeks later, on the night of 6 July 1944, when 4000 Japanese troops launched a huge banzai suicide charge against the Americans. Three days later many of those left alive committed suicide by jumping from the cliffs at Marpi Point. Significantly, for the first time in the war it was not just soldiers and sailors who killed themselves but civilians as well – including thousands of women and children. 'They would get the child in their arms, and they'd bend over and jump off the cliff,' says Michael Witowich, who was on patrol nearby. 'They'd jump and you could hear the screaming of the children on the coral.' Seeing the children waiting to leap to their deaths, he decided to act: 'I used to shoot the children as they went down, so they wouldn't suffer when they hit the coral. I used to think in my dreams whether it was right for me to do that, so they wouldn't have to suffer when they went down. 'Cos when they hit the coral they'd still be alive and have a horrible death, so it's like shooting a horse that breaks its leg – and this is a human being.'

The civilian suicides on Saipan marked a turning point. Up to that moment suicide had essentially been the prerogative of the military, or of senior figures within the Japanese elite. Now, fuelled by the desperate knowledge that their soldiers must not be taken alive, thousands of ordinary civilians took their own lives. The Japanese army on the island played a key role in encouraging civilians to die, convincing them that it would be shameful to survive the occupation of the island and that the Americans would torture, rape or kill them if they were captured alive.

Japanese propaganda films made shortly after the loss of Saipan emphasize the nobility of dying in the struggle against the Allies, and the message was spread even amongst Japanese schoolchildren. 'We have heard that all our soldiers on Saipan died bravely,' shouts an army officer to a parade ground full of solemn-faced young children in one newsreel. 'All the Japanese civilians on the island cooperated with the army and shared their fate.' The propaganda did not trumpet the reality – that for the first time in the conflict Japanese pre-war territory had fallen and that as a result Tojo had resigned (to be replaced by Kuniaki Koiso, who survived as prime minister until April 1945). Instead, it proselytized the fiction that there can be glory in defeat if it is marked by self-sacrifice for the good of the nation, the good of the emperor. The desire for the last elusive 'victory' was becoming corrupted into the belief that defeat could become victory if the enemy took the land but not its people.

It was this attitude that was to influence the creation of the most uniquely Japanese military unit of the war – the kamikaze ('divine wind') – and it was during the battle of Saipan that the seeds were sown for the birth of these institutionalized suicide squads. On 19 June 1944, in the seas around Saipan, the Japanese air force lost a total of 315 aircraft to the Allies. It was obvious that Allied military technology had progressed so quickly that the advantage the Japanese Zero fighter had possessed in the early days of the war had evaporated. Six weeks later in Tokyo, Warrant Officer Shoichi Ota believed he had come up with a solution to the problem. He showed a drawing of a missile he had conceived to design technician Tadanao Miki. Incredibly, Ota's plan called for a missile to be slung underneath a bomber and then piloted the last few miles to its target by a human being. 'I was amazed,' says Miki. 'I thought, "Who's going to pilot it?" As an engineer I was against it. I felt a person's life could not be regarded so lightly. But then Ota said, "I would pilot it." That's what he said. And I thought, "Oh my God!"'[7] As a result of Ota's personal commitment to the project, the missile was put into production.

At the same time as Ota's missile was being built, Japanese pilots were showing that they too, without specific orders, could sense the mood of the nation. On 20 August the Ozuki fighter unit was sent into action against American bombers approaching the home islands of Japan. 'During the dogfight,' says Masaji Kobayashi, who flew on the sortie, 'two pilots suddenly announced that they were out of bullets and were going to crash into the B-29s. I saw two of them deliberately crash their planes into the B-29s. It was not planned but spontaneous.' Just as with the sacrifice at Saipan, Japanese newspapers proclaimed that this airborne suicide attack was proof that spiritual strength was every bit as potent as military power. But Japanese commanders (especially Vice Admiral Takijiro Onishi) realized that, outnumbered as they were, it was nothing more than a gesture to sacrifice one Japanese plane for an American one. If this suicide tactic was to have military as opposed to propaganda value, the target would have to be more significant. And there was nothing more threatening to Japan than the American aircraft

carriers — the warships that had, from the Japanese perspective, so trag-
ically escaped destruction at Pearl Harbor.

As a result, in October 1944, as the Allied fleet approached the
Philippines, and with Ota's piloted missile not yet ready, the elite
Japanese 201st Air Group was given a new task. Volunteers were called
for, and told that their mission would be to fly a plane packed with
explosives directly into an Allied carrier. It was the job of Wing
Commander Tadashi Nakajima to explain the new plan to the assembled
pilots: 'I said, "Those who volunteer please write down your names on a
piece of paper." I wondered. What would I do if nobody did? But that
evening an officer brought all the scraps of paper to me. In the whole
unit only three had not volunteered.' The three who had not put their
names down were in the unit hospital. Every able-bodied pilot had said
he was prepared to die — some had even signed the request form with
their own blood. 'Later that night,' recalls Nakajima, 'one of the officers
said, "You asked the rank and file, but you didn't ask us." I replied, "I
didn't ask you because I *knew* you would volunteer." And the officer
smiled. He was very happy to hear that.'

On 25 October 1944, aircraft of the Japanese 201st Air Group left
their base in the Philippines to mount suicide attacks on Allied carrier
groups just over 400 miles (650 km) away. 'I had just finished breakfast,'
says Robert Fentriss, one of the American sailors in the carrier group
targeted by these first kamikazes, 'and about that time the general alarm
went, bong-bong, and then there was the rat-a-tat-tat-tat of machine
guns and then WHOOM, that was it. And in just a fraction of a second
the ship was in a roaring inferno. There was smoke and you couldn't see
— all sorts of confusion.'

'I watched this plane come in,' says John Mitchell, a gunner's mate
on a nearby US warship, 'and it just kept coming in. It was like slow
motion almost, because he was firing his guns. I almost saw the projec-
tiles hitting the deck. And the plane kept coming in and it didn't pull
out. And I yelled, "Pull out, you bastard, pull out!"'

The US carrier *Santee* was severely damaged by the kamikaze
attacks. But such was the shock and disbelief amongst the American

sailors that it was not until the next day that they fully understood that the Japanese were mounting a mass, planned suicide attack. 'I was just absolutely dumbfounded,' says Robert Fentriss. 'I could not believe that someone would do something like that. I couldn't believe what I had seen. And I said to one of my shipmates who was standing very close to me, "Did you see what that joker did?" or words to that effect. That's the first time I knew it was a kamikaze.' 'We were a really cocky bunch,' says Bill Simmons, another US sailor in the same carrier group. 'We thought we had the war won. And then when they began the kamikaze attacks, it just scared the living daylights out of everybody. Suddenly we were not the great navy we felt we were.'

The action of the kamikaze pilots was inexplicable to these American sailors. After all, wasn't the whole point of fighting in a war to try to survive it? But the Japanese pilots had been educated in a wholly different philosophy. At the core of it was not just the belief that their supreme commander, Emperor Hirohito, was a divine figure whose orders must be obeyed without question, but the spiritual faith that after death as kamikaze pilots their souls would dwell in the emperor's own shrine. 'Everybody at that time knew that their soul would go back to Yasukini,' says Morimasa Yunokawa, then a pilot in the Japanese navy. 'That was the special place where the souls of those who had died fighting for the country and their emperor went.' Propaganda archive of the time shows war widows visiting the Yasukini shrine across from the Imperial Palace in Tokyo, so that, as the commentary puts it, 'they can at last meet again those who have been living on only in their memories. For the widows, this was an unforgettable moment to show their appreciation for being able to honour their god-like husbands.'

However, it is important for those of us in the West who have been brought up with the concept of Christian martyrdom to realize that the spiritual beliefs of the kamikaze were not analogous. The focus of the kamikaze pilots was at least as much on the service they were doing to the society they left behind than on the certainty of an afterlife. 'There is no living thing that desires death,' says Hachiro Hosokawa, another Japanese wartime pilot. 'But there comes a time when you face responsibilities you cannot run away from, and at that point you give up your life. To give up your life for your country and your people was the highest honour. It was not only me but everyone who thought that way.' In a country where the group mattered more than the individual, there could be no higher glory than to die in such a suicide attack.

Despite the kamikazes, the 'one great victory' that Hirohito and the Japanese High Command were chasing was still proving elusive. Their plan was not proving to be a strategy so much as wishful thinking – and wishful thinking began to be the order of the day. In early October 1944, Hirohito's advisers simply misled him – they told him that overall, in a series of sea engagements, the Japanese had won great victories and that sixteen American carriers had been sunk (in reality the Imperial Navy had not sunk one of them). It was this kind of false briefing that led Hirohito to suppose that a decisive victory over the Americans could be won as the enemy approached Leyte in the Philippines later that month. Yet again, the Japanese leadership were chasing a dream. Between 22 and 27 October the Americans inflicted another massive defeat at Leyte Gulf, sinking four Japanese carriers and killing more than 10,000 Japanese servicemen. The superior firepower of the Americans had proved decisive once again.

Meantime, on the Southeast Asian mainland the British (with Indian army soldiers playing a prominent part) managed to defeat the Imperial Army on the Northeastern border of India at the battles of Imphal and Kohima and in the process the Japanese 15th army was almost completely destroyed. During the autumn of 1944 the Allied forces pushed the remaining Japanese back towards Burma, with Colonel Orde Wingate's guerilla Chindits harrying them from behind the lines.

As autumn turned to winter in 1944 the Japanese were facing something unique in their long history as a nation – catastrophic defeat. Starting the war had been easy. Ending it – before the whole of Japan was in ruins – would prove more difficult.

ENDGAME

By the start of 1945 the Japanese leadership were trapped in the near impossible situation they had created for themselves. Militarily they knew they must be defeated – but they could not surrender unconditionally because that would mean the destruction of the whole emperor system, and life without that was inconceivable. There were precious few alternatives; the easy option was to keep fighting and hope for the best – perhaps the Americans would eventually falter in the face of suicidal Japanese resistance. Unfortunately for the Japanese, by the start of 1945 it was clear that this option was also the one least likely to succeed. But how else could the impossible circle be squared – how could they surrender without sacrificing the emperor?

One possibility, some of Hirohito's advisers thought, was to persuade him to abdicate in favour of his son, the eleven-year-old crown prince. To that end secret discussions were held in January 1945 with the chief abbot of Ninnaji temple to see if it might be possible for Hirohito to 'retire' to a temple in Kyoto. But the talks came to nothing – it was still easier and more comforting for the Japanese elite to put their faith in the fantasy of the 'one big victory and then peace' strategy.

In February 1945, as the Japanese leadership procrastinated, American marines landed on the tiny volcanic island of Iwo Jima, less than 700 miles (1100 km) south of Tokyo. The island was a vital strategic objective for the Allies, as use of its airstrips would allow bombing raids to be mounted more effectively against the home islands of Japan. Once more the Japanese response was tenacious and desperate. Beneath the sulphurous landscape the defenders, under the command of Lieutenant General Tadamichi Kuribayahi, built a honeycomb of tunnels and

fox-holes. Their fierce defence of the island cost the Americans dear —
by the time it was captured, after a five-week battle, one in three of the
marines who had taken part had been killed or wounded.

The level of sacrifice made by the marines on Iwo Jima had a profound effect not just on public opinion in the United States but also on
their fellow servicemen in the Pacific. Weeks after the island had been
taken, Paul Montgomery and the rest of his bomber crew landed on Iwo
Jima to refuel on their way back to base on the island of Tinian: 'We
were taxiing in and I passed right by a graveyard. There were an indescribable number of marker crosses. I couldn't describe to you how
affected I was. I had never seen 7000 markers before. And when I came
to realize that they were just kids like myself and that they wouldn't be
going home…. It just took something out of me that I didn't know was
there. I thought I was pretty tough. I wasn't tough. I became traumatized
with the price that had been paid for that island — and the reason they
took it was so I could have a runway to land on coming back.'

Paul Montgomery was just one of thousands of young Americans
participating during the spring and summer of 1945 in the biggest aerial
bombardment in history. Early in the war the Americans had attempted
to use precision bombing against Japanese military and industrial targets, but in January 1945 that policy changed with the arrival of a new
air force commander — General Curtis Le May. The new tactic was
simple — burn whole cities to the ground. In an effort to force Japan to
accept unconditional surrender (and eradicate the need for more
marines to die capturing islands like Iwo Jima) the decision had been
taken to bring the war home to the civilian population in a cataclysmic
manner. Packed with incendiaries, B-29 bombers now flew low over
Japanese towns at night and set the buildings on fire.

The controversy over the decision to use nuclear bombs at
Hiroshima and Nagasaki has overshadowed Le May's earlier devastating
conventional bombing campaign against Japan. As a result, one astounding fact has not seeped into the public consciousness — five months
before the atomic bombs were dropped, on the night of 10 March 1945,
the Americans fire-bombed Tokyo and killed around 100,000 in the

biggest fire storm in history. More people died in a few hours than in either of the later attacks with atomic bombs.

'I remember there was no alarm or air raid warning,' says Yoshiko Hashimoto, then a young mother in Tokyo. 'But the sky in the west was blazing red, scarlet red, like a bright sunset burning. Usually B-29s flying at high altitude looked small, but these B-29s looked gigantic, looming very close and dispersing their bombs. And it was almost like a heavy evening shower coming down.'

The fire was so intense that it became obvious to Yoshiko's father and mother that they and their three daughters had to leave the air raid shelter and seek another place of safety. 'I knew we had to flee,' she says, 'but we had to take some things with us – there was a dire shortage of everything to wear or to sleep on. So my mother and father and sisters went into the house and put the bedding mattress and clothes on a hand cart. And I was told that since I had a baby I had to escape first. Right next to my house there was a big avenue and the fire was coming close by, like a blizzard of fire – yes, a blizzard of fire. We couldn't keep our eyes open, wind was blowing the debris from the fire all around.'

Yoshiko picked up her baby and hurried down towards the elevated railway line that ran above the street to wait for the rest of her family. When they arrived her father said the railway might be a target for further bombing so they decided to run in the direction of the river. Around them was pandemonium. 'There were so many people seeking refuge, moving in various directions. The paths and roads were packed – from the narrow alley to the big road. Everybody was panicked, pushing around. Everybody was trying to call for each other and we heard the children starting to scream.'

One of Yoshiko's sisters was running holding a big pot of rice – as precious as gold in those times of starvation – and so could not hold her parents' hands as she ran. 'She was pushed around by the crowd and was swaying and faltering. I was very worried about her. I kept on calling to her. But gradually the distance between me and her grew bigger and I lost sight of her. It's very sad. She was eighteen and had pony tails. Still my youngest sister is eighteen – I lost her.'

The rest of the Hashimoto family pressed on through the throng until they reached the river. They were surrounded by fire. 'I saw living people burnt alive,' says Yoshiko. 'People one by one were quickly burning to death, struggling and suffering.' The bedding mattresses that many had saved from their houses proved deadly liabilities as they caught fire and burned amongst the crowd. Across the river warehouses were ablaze. The screams of the victims mingled with the acrid smell of smoke and burning, all lit in a hellish flame-orange glow. 'I heard a very sharp scream on my back – it was my baby! And I turned around and he was crying with his mouth open so that little powdery pieces of fire got into his mouth. And my mother screamed that I should get him in my arms, get him off my back. So I held him in my arms while my mother and father tried to protect themselves from the raging fire.' Witnessing the nightmare scenes around him, Yoshiko's father shouted to his daughter to jump into the river. 'But in March it was very cold,' she says, 'and I didn't have courage to jump at first. And besides I had my baby in my arms.... So I was hesitating, and I kept on hesitating, and my mother also said, "Jump in!" And I was almost scolded. In her eyes they didn't have any hope of life, but my son was the only hope for her – he was her first grandson. She adored him very much. So I decided to jump into the river with my baby in my arms. When I jumped in I heard the sound of fire in my clothes being extinguished. And the water was extremely cold. Looking around on the surface of the river there were many who had jumped before me.' On the bank stood her father and mother – neither of them could follow their daughter and grandson into the water. Her father had an injury to his leg and her mother had never learnt to swim. 'They probably burnt to death there,' says Yoshiko. 'Both my mother and father would have caught fire and died. It's very painful even to think of that.'

Once she was in the river Yoshiko tried to cling to passing logs but they were slippery and she saw people pushed under the water as the logs turned. Eventually she hung on to a passing raft and managed to put her baby on top of it. She was lucky – other mothers who had jumped in with their babies on their backs, rather than holding them in their arms as she had done, turned round and saw that their children had drowned: 'The mothers' heads are above the water but the babies on their backs are under the water – so the babies died without the mothers knowing. These young mothers just lost their minds when they saw what had happened.'

As she clung to the raft, knowing she could not survive much longer in the cold water, Yoshiko saw a small rowing boat approaching, with two young men pulling at the oars: 'They passed the raft, and shamelessly I shouted and asked for help – if not for me then just for my son. They rowed close to me and dragged my son and me on to the boat.' She spent the rest of the night on the small boat as around her Tokyo burned. 'Everywhere we saw burnt corpses and [heard] the screams and cries of pain and torment.' In places the surface of the water – covered with wood and oil – had caught fire, but still people jumped in from the banks and the bridges. 'Everyone jumped in that sea of fire and many were chanting the Buddhist *sutra* – but you cannot be calm there.'

The next morning they were able to land upstream, and Yoshiko took her baby to hospital. 'The doctor gave my son a big sedative shot and at long last he started drinking water. The I realized that my son was alive and that was a tremendous sense of relief. And then I wept.' Around her, on the way to the hospital, she had been astonished at the destruction. 'There wasn't anyone alive – everyone had been burnt to death. Not a living soul. It was beyond belief. And everything was burnt so that you could see all the way, almost to the horizon. The town and community you were born and lived in simply reduced to ashes. I still have this nightmare – the burnt corpses of people looking like withered trees. I saw mothers that died trying to protect their children – I saw them.' That night Yoshiko lost her mother, father and one of her sisters. 'Many, many civilians were killed,' she says. 'The atomic bombs were terrible, but conventional weapons also bring death to many, many people. Fifty years after the war, I met a pilot of a B-29 bomber and I asked him, "As you were raiding Tokyo, dropping bombs, did you ever think that, underneath you, my parents and many others were being killed?" And he said, "It's a very difficult question to answer."'

When the same question was put to Paul Montgomery, who as a member of an American B-29 bomb crew took part in many of the fire-bomb raids of 1945, his answer was simple and straightforward: 'I didn't have any feelings at the time. I guess the reason I didn't was that I wanted to get the war over. I was insensitive to the bombing of the cities. I really was wanting to get the war over and I wanted to get home. And if they told me to go bomb cities, I went and bombed cities.' Montgomery – in common with the rest of the American air crews – knew that his mission now was not to attack industrial targets but to destroy civilian life, even to the extent of deliberately trying to hinder the work of the firemen who would try and extinguish the blaze: 'We dropped 100-pound phosphorus bombs, and in that bomb cluster there were anti-firefighting bombs that would go off at unspecified times – upon impact, six hours later, the next day.' The only time Montgomery felt substantial contact with the people whose lives he was destroying was when he participated in the fire-bombing of Kure, a town in the southwest of the main Japanese island of Honshu: 'We came in from the inland sea – it's a coastal town. And I could not find any area that was not already afire – we were one of the last ones in. Kure was burning with such intensity and we were at such low level – we weren't pressurized – that obnoxious odours from the incineration came up to our airplane. There was such an odour of human waste coming up that I was gagging. I opened the escape hatch to see if the bomb bay was cleared and that odour struck me as an indescribable stench – somewhere between burning urine and human waste. We finally found an area of Kure that wasn't on fire and we dropped the bombs – but it was a nauseating experience.' But even this did not make Montgomery feel compassion for the civilians whose lives he was taking. 'I felt everything except mercy for the people. I was not obsessed with any feeling of sympathy – I just wasn't. I was young and I was case-hardened. I had a kind of cast-iron attitude towards war. I had lost my sensitivity, evidently.'

Crucial to the ability of men like Paul Montgomery to escape feelings of compassion for the women and children they were incinerating was the distancing effect of aerial bombardment: 'It's not like I was going out and sticking a bayonet in someone's belly, okay? You still kill them but you kill them from a distance, and it doesn't have the demoralizing effect upon you that it did if I went up and stuck a bayonet in someone's stomach in the course of combat. It's just different. It's kind of like conducting war through a video game, if you will.' But Montgomery and his colleagues were not completely immune from understanding that there was a difference between bombing a military base and bombing a school or hospital. 'We didn't talk about bombing the cities – there was just no conversation about it. Mitsubishi – yes, the factories – yes, the naval bases – yes, Yokohama, gasoline refineries – yes. But the cities, there was a kind of deadly silence there. Everybody felt – it was women and children – but it was never spoken. It was just never spoken. Even today when we have a reunion, the bombing of the cities isn't mentioned. We talk about the military targets but we don't talk about the bombing of the cities – it's just kind of off limits.'

Paul Montgomery was brought up in a deeply religious family, and still today it is obvious that he is a caring, kind man. And that is ultimately what is so disturbing about his testimony. This man who was capable of shedding tears when he saw the grave markers of US marines on Iwo Jima – a sight that still causes him to break down as he describes it today – remains unmoved by his participation in the mass killing of thousands upon thousands of Japanese women and children. His testimony is a powerful reminder of the morally numbing effect of war conducted by modern technological means.

Emperor Hirohito made a rare trip from his palace in central Tokyo (one of the few buildings that had escaped the firestorm) to tour the sections of the capital devastated by the bombing. His reaction to the destruction and suffering was true to form; he called, yet again, for one last decisive victory that would enable the Japanese to negotiate with the Allies from a position of relative strength.

In March 1945, the same month as the Tokyo fire-bombing, the suicide missile conceived by Shoichi Ota was ready to be used against the Allied fleet for the first time. Perhaps, military leaders felt, these special kamikazes, named the Jin-rai Butai, the 'Thunder Gods', would prove to be the secret weapon that would turn the war for the Japanese. Those who had volunteered to fly Ota's missile gathered near Tokyo at the

Kanaiki training base. Today some of the few survivors of the unit (who most often escaped death because their planes or missiles failed technically before their target was reached) confess that they did not embark on their mission with quite the insouciance presented on the propaganda newsreels. 'We all brooded constantly on our death,' says Hachiro Hosokawa. 'In the Ohka missile death was certain, and we were simply waiting for our time to come. And the waiting seemed to go on for ever. It was like being sentenced to death – as though you were waiting for the electric chair.' 'I started to wonder whether when I had volunteered I had been in my right mind,' says Fujio Hayashi, another of the Thunder Gods. 'And whether, when the time actually came for us to depart, I would tremble, that my hands would shake. It would have been a disgrace for a Japanese to act like that.'

That March the first group of Thunder Gods were launched against the Allied fleet south of the home islands of Japan. Eighteen bombers took off and headed out over the sea. With the Ohka missile strapped beneath them, the bombers were slow and vulnerable. When they were still far from their targets, American fighters intercepted them and shot every one down. All these first volunteers were killed without taking any of the enemy with them. Ironically, Shoichi Ota, the inventor of this supposed wonder weapon, was not on the raid. He had not reached the required standard as a pilot. 'At the base,' says Fujio Hayashi, 'Ota came up to me and said, "I'm sorry it's such a poor weapon. I wasn't thinking of something like that, but of something which had a much higher capability." He said again he was very sorry.'

After this disaster it was clear that the longed-for decisive victory would not be bought by the Thunder Gods. But that spring the emperor and the rest of the Japanese High Command had another straw at which to grasp – the Imperial Army dug in on the island of Okinawa. Once again, the Imperial Army and Navy were ordered to make a heroic stand and win a great victory.

At first, the defiant way in which the Japanese intended to secure that victory was not evident to the Allies. On 1 April 50,000 US troops landed on beaches on the western side of the island. The Americans expected the Japanese to defend the landing ground, but the marines were virtually unopposed. 'Everyone was very happy,' says James Eagleton, then with the US Marine Corps. 'What happened to the Japanese? We just thought we were luckier than hell. And we were very surprised that there wasn't cannon fire, mortar fire, small arms fire meeting us. We were very pleased.'

Similarly, the Allied fleet off Okinawa sailed virtually untroubled until the afternoon of 6 April. Then, suddenly, out of a clear sky came wave upon wave of kamikazes. 'It was a saturation-type thing,' says Frank Manson, a US navy communications officer. 'I mean there was one kamikaze, and then there was two, and then three, and they'd just keep coming.' For the first time kamikaze pilots were attacking in large groups of over thirty planes at a time, in a tactic known as *kikusui* or Floating Chrysanthemums. 'The way we stopped them was just to fill the air with flak,' says Bill Simmons, another US sailor who endured the kamikaze attacks off Okinawa. 'And if there was ever an opening in the flak they were on you. And we had a number of them just barely miss us.' 'Eventually, of course, we knew they'd get us,' says Frank Manson, 'but we hoped, and I think our gunners hoped, that they'd shoot down enough of them that they might pick another target.'

It was not just American warships that suffered kamikaze attacks off Okinawa. Several British ships were hit as well. 'I think it was the worst moment of my life,' says Ronald Hay, a fighter pilot who served on one of the British carriers during the battle. 'I'd been frightened many times in the war, but that was about the worst time. Sitting there knowing that one kamikaze coming in there could have swept the whole of our complement of aircraft and aircrew into the sea – maybe kill the whole lot. It's not nice. We wouldn't have expected to survive if a kamikaze had hit the deck. All of us would have gone up smoke. There would have been a lot of roasting going on.'

Hay was lucky – he was able to lead his squadron into the sky before a kamikaze hit them as they lay vulnerable, fuelled and armed, waiting to take off. Once airborne, he and his colleagues found that the kamikaze planes were easy to destroy: 'You'd only got to do a short burst and these matchwood planes would explode or collapse – very silly little planes, you might think. You should never go to war in those sorts of things – they had no armour plate protection. It wasn't difficult to shoot them down. Many of them were not really good pilots and they missed everything and plunged straight into the sea – what a waste.' Hay and his colleagues found little to admire or respect in their adversaries. 'Because of what we'd heard about what they did in the land fighting we had no compassion for them at all. The only good Japanese were dead ones – that was our philosophy. We thought they were the most outrageously ghastly, horrible people.'

Despite the poor quality of their aircraft, the massed kamikaze attacks off Okinawa were effective – altogether twenty-four American ships were sunk and around 200 were damaged. And the psychological strain of facing wave upon wave of kamikazes also took its toll: 'We had one gunner whose 40-millimetre guns had been hit,' says US navy veteran John Mitchell, 'and he just simply got up on his gun and jumped over the side, and someone heard him say, "It's hot today." And he jumped right into the water and we never saw or heard from him again.'

When Ronnie Hay returned from one sortie he found that his ship had been damaged by a kamikaze attack: 'One of them hit the port forward gun turret and that killed about six people and maybe injured another six. And the second one bounced right off the flight deck aft and that swept a few airplanes into the sea and killed maybe eight people. And all they do is to brush the remains over the side. That's all they can do. And that's how we buried our friends – I mean, there were only bits and pieces left.'

The British ships with their armoured decks were much less susceptible to kamikaze attacks than the American carriers which had wooden ones. If a single kamikaze hit the centre of the flight deck of an American carrier it could penetrate to the decks below and place the ship in extreme danger. So the Americans lived in particular fear of the kamikazes – a fact that helps to place in context the extraordinary actions of Fred Murphy, an engineering officer on one of the US warships, when some weeks after a kamikaze attack he visited one of his ship's holds to investigate a malfunctioning fuel oil indicator: 'I was digging through to get to this vertical pipe and I came across what turned out to be this kamikaze pilot's leg, his right leg. And it had been blown off about halfway up from the knee and of course it was all black, 'cause it was burnt, and it was about a month and a half later so everything was pretty rotten. And guys were souvenir-happy by that time — anything you could find that was Japanese they'd make souvenirs out of it. So I took this, and of course it still had some meat on it —and as I tell it now it sounds kind of gruesome. And really it's bad, it sounds bad, but I was young and hardened by the war and it didn't bother me at all to pick it up and take it up there and say, "Here — make some souvenirs out of it." The guys actually sliced up the bones into cross-sections. They made necklaces and bones of that pilot.' Only in 'recent years' has it occurred to Fred Murphy that 'if the parents of that boy — that young airman — knew that we took the leg of their son and did that, it would be terrible.' But, he feels, 'at the same time it doesn't detract from the fact that he was trying to kill us and we were trying to kill him, right? So I didn't feel guilty — there's no guilt about it. It's just a feeling of sadness that men will do things like that, you know.'

The kamikazes kept attacking the Allied fleet, and every day that spring and early summer Fujio Hayashi had to select pilots from the list of volunteers to fly on these missions: 'I kept putting my own name on the list but they'd strike it off. They preferred me to continue selecting the pilots instead. Lieutenant Nakajima would give the order and then they would walk away up the steep bamboo hill up to the very top where the airport was. Then they would go to the runway where the planes were on standby. I never saw any more because it was too painful, and I would run in the opposite direction to a place no one else ever went. I would squat down and I would cry. The runway was high up above and I could hear them singing as they went to it. I can remember the song: "Our golden flower on our flying caps shines as bright as our high spirits. Oh, blue sky! Great sky! You welcome us brave pilots to you."'

The image of noble — entirely voluntary — self-sacrifice that Hayashi describes is almost as seductive today as it was to the Japanese who saw the story replayed countless times on the propaganda newsreels. But, as the testimony of Kenichiro Oonuki reveals, such images are not the whole truth. Given the pressure to conform in Japanese society, it is rare to find an individual who is prepared to speak out against the prevailing sentiment about the war – rarer still to find that quality in a man trained to be a kamikaze pilot, which is why our interview with him was especially valuable.

In 1943 Oonuki joined the imperial armed forces and underwent pilot training: 'The young people at that time had a sense of longing about being a pilot,' he says. 'I thought being a pilot may be interesting – so it was a simple motivation. Nobody dreamt that this kind of sad ending was awaiting.'

Shortly after the first kamikaze attacks off the Philippines in October 1944, all the pilots at Oonuki's training base were called to a meeting. A senior officer told them that recruitment was currently taking place for a 'special mission', and that if they volunteered they should be clear that there was no possibility of surviving it. The pilots were told that they should think over whether they wished to volunteer for the mission or not, and the next morning each should answer in one of three ways: 'No', 'Yes' or 'Yes, I volunteer with all my heart.'

That night the pilots discussed amongst themselves what they should do. One of them, on behalf of the whole group, went and asked the senior officer to describe this 'special mission' in more detail. He was told that all the pilots who volunteered would be asked to crash their planes into enemy warships. Again, it was emphasized that survival was impossible. 'We were taken aback,' says Oonuki. 'I felt it was not the type of mission I would willingly apply for.' He was happy to face the possibility – even the probability – of death as a pilot, but this 'certain death' seemed 'ridiculous'. All the other pilots agreed with him and 'nobody was really willing to go'. But then they started working through the consequences of refusing to 'volunteer'. They thought it certain they would be accused of cowardice and subjected to that most terrifying of punishments for a Japanese – shame and ostracism from the group. Then this verdict would be reported to their families, and they too would be punished with ostracism, condemned to be shunned by all other Japanese. 'I've heard of many cases such as this in the past,' says Oonuki. It was a fate that none of them wished to bring on the families they loved. Then, as they sat talking through the night, another likely consequence of refusing to volunteer occurred to them. Those who did not become kamikazes would most likely be 'isolated and then sent to the forefront of the most severe battle and meet a sure death anyway'. As a result of this careful, logical thought process, next morning every pilot volunteered to become a kamikaze, all signing that they freely put themselves forward 'with all their heart'. 'Nobody wanted to,' says Oonuki, 'but everybody did.'

Kenichiro Oonuki's testimony offers a hugely revealing insight into the mentality not just of the kamikazes, but of many Japanese during the war. His frank comments render inadequate the Westernized notion of the mindless fanaticism of the Japanese, and explode the idea that the Japanese are somehow 'inscrutable' or devoid of feelings with which Westerners can readily empathize. The dilemma that Oonuki and his comrades faced that night, as they sat and decided whether they should 'volunteer', is readily understandable to everyone who hears it – as is their subsequent decision to become kamikazes. In fact, given the circumstances, the exceptional person would have been the one who did not volunteer. An idea of how these rare individuals who stood out against the group were perceived by those in authority is given by Tadashi Nakajima, a commander in the Imperial Navy who was involved, as he puts it, in 'kamikaze administration'. 'One lieutenant didn't want to become a kamikaze pilot,' he says. 'He came over and told me so. And as a result he was going to be transferred. Then the American enemy came, all of a sudden, so we all ran. After the enemy planes had gone we reassembled for a head-count. There was one person missing – and it was this lieutenant. He had been shot through the neck and killed. Every single other person was alive except this man who had gone to ask for a transfer. It's very strange, isn't it?' The unfortunate lieutenant who did not volunteer to be a kamikaze was dead within minutes – but how much longer would he have lasted even if the Americans had not appeared? He was almost certainly going to be 'transferred' to a front-line squadron where he would have had little hope of survival. Kenichiro Oonuki and his comrades were surely right – not to volunteer could still be a route to death.

Tadashi Nakajima says he felt little pity for the young pilots whom he sent on suicide missions: 'I've studied Zen a little bit, and in Zen life and death do not exist. And so just because a person dies a little before you, the difference is really unimportant if you think of life and death on a Zen timescale – the timescale of the universe.'

The fact that 'on the timescale of the universe' it was not important that they were all to die young was not much comfort to Kenichiro Oonuki and his comrades as they embarked on a conversion course to turn them from conventional pilots into kamikazes. They spent some weeks training in 'rapid descent towards the ground' and 'nose diving'. Practising to crash was extremely dangerous, because if they 'made a little mistake there's no possibility of correcting the altitude of the plane. I saw many die during the training. And if you hit the ground,' says Oonuki, 'it's very difficult to collect up the pieces of the bodies.' In the spring of 1945 they were told their training was over and they were to take part in the kamikaze attack on the Allied fleet off Okinawa.

By now Oonuki was at peace with himself: 'When you come to the last stage you have a sense of resignation.' The night before his squadron of a dozen kamikazes was due to depart 'there was a lot of sake, but nobody could feel cheerful – we went to bed at about nine.' The next morning he went to check his aircraft and was told that because of mechanical problems his plane could not fly – indeed, only half of the squadron, six planes, were in a fit state to leave at the appointed time of 3.30 in the afternoon. Oonuki was disappointed – he wanted to die not alongside strangers but alongside the comrades with whom he had trained. That afternoon, as six of his colleagues prepared to leave he went up to them as their engines were running and gave them each a bouquet of azaleas. 'And one comrade said, "I am going ahead of you. I wanted to meet my destiny with you – I'm sorry." Everybody had the same expression in their eyes, like a deep-sea fish looking up at the blue sky above. I've never seen sadder expressions in anyone's eyes since then.'

Two days later, on 5 April 1945, it was finally Kenichiro Oonuki's turn to leave. His plane repaired, he flew off with another kamikaze squadron towards Okinawa. But *en route* his plane developed engine problems and he had to land on a Japanese-occupied island and effect repairs. The next day he and three other kamikazes flew on again, but twenty minutes' flying time from Okinawa they were attacked by American fighters and the other kamikazes were shot down. 'Right in front of me my colleagues died,' he says. 'When they fall it's almost like a little chunk of stone. The Americans kept on attacking and I made a rapid turn and tried to escape and then my plane was hit. It was a tremendous shock – almost like you're beaten by a fist.' His plane was losing oil rapidly from a lubricant tank, but by a great piece of good fortune he was able to make an emergency landing on one of the smaller Ryukyu islands. 'It was a miraculous landing,' he says. 'There were pot-holes all over the runway – and if I'd hit a pothole the plane would have toppled over and I would have died.' Left on the island with a disabled plane he felt a 'sense of dishonour' that he had not been able to complete his suicide mission. After ten days a Japanese ship arrived at the island and Oonuki began a tortuous journey back to the home islands of Japan. Once back at base he and a selection of other kamikaze pilots who had failed in their mission were berated: 'The commanding officer and the general staff officer came out, and the first thing they said was, "Why did you come back?" We thought that they would say, "You've had a tough time. Have a rest and we'll give you another plane to join a new kamikaze mission." But we were all reprimanded, scolded.' Oonuki and his comrades were confined to quarters and brutally treated: 'I was beaten with a bamboo sword and for two days I was in bed – I couldn't move at all. And many others had to go through that. Some broke the glass window and tried to kill themselves, but we saved them.'

At the end of the war Oonuki and the rest of the failed kamikaze pilots were released from the isolation of their imprisonment, but he did not talk about his experience until relatively recently: 'We who survived felt a deep sense of guilt. Your colleagues with whom you felt a stronger bond almost than with your own family had died, and you had simply survived. In captivity it was a very painful experience, with the mental torture of being called disloyal and a coward, and if we had disclosed what had happened that would have been another dishonour to us.' Now, looking back on all his experiences as a kamikaze, Oonuki has formed a straightforward view about the worth of these 'special attack missions': 'It was folly, reckless. It was simply ridiculous.'

Those who watched the propaganda newsreels were invited to form a very different opinion. One typical film shows kamikaze pilots waiting to be sent on a mission being read a special message from Hirohito: 'These words are from the Emperor,' they are told. 'Those who attacked the enemy individually have done a great job and produced remarkable results. How brave they were to sacrifice their lives for their country.' Their commanding officer then goes on to say that 'the Emperor has ordered us to pass his sincere sympathies to the late families of the deceased and to their colleagues on the front line.' After this message one of the kamikaze pilots on parade salutes and says: 'I would like to thank the Emperor on behalf of us all. We are so proud and impressed that the Emperor himself sent us such words. We promise to accomplish our mission as bravely as our predecessors.'

The effect of such propaganda was profound. The central message – that the divine emperor himself was wholly in favour of suicide attacks – was simple and had an inescapable impact. 'I thought they [the kamikazes] were doing very well,' says Shigeaki Kinjou, who was in his teens at the time. 'I believed that they were sacrificing their lives for the country. And civilians, we should also be ready to sacrifice our lives for the country when the time came.'

Kinjou lived on the small island of Tokashiki, a few miles from Okinawa. In March 1945, the Americans landed on Tokashiki and started to move inland. Immediately the Japanese army issued hand grenades to some of the villagers. Significantly they gave out two to each person – one to throw at the Americans and the other to blow themselves up. Just as at Saipan, the army told the islanders that they

Above Kenichiro Oonuki in a defiant pose, symbolic of the propaganda image of the Kamikaze pilot. But belying the popular myth of willing self-sacrifice, Oonuki and his comrades volunteered knowing that the idea of dying in a suicide attack was 'ridiculous'.

Opposite top An American carrier is hit by kamikaze attack in the spring of 1944. The flight decks of the American carriers were made of wood, and so a hit like this was potentially devastating, with the fire quickly spreading to the decks below.

Opposite left One of nearly 400 Japanese planes shot down during an attack on the Allied fleet off the Marianas in June 1944.

Opposite right Emperor Hirohito leaves the Yasukini Shrine near the Imperial Palace in Tokyo, after paying his respects to Japanese war dead killed in the war in China.

Right In Arizona, the girlfriend of an American serviceman fighting in New Guinea, writes a thank-you note to her boyfriend for sending her a Japanese skull signed by his comrades.

Below A marine cemetery in Iwo Jima at the foot of Mount Suribachi. It was the sight of thousands of crosses like these that so affected US flyer Paul Montgomery (see p. 114).

Left One of the thousands of Japanese families torn apart by the fire-bombing of Tokyo on 9 March 1945. Yoshiko Hashimoto (top row, first from right) lost her father (bottom row, left) and mother (top row, middle) and only survived herself thanks to a piece of luck (see p. 116).

Below As the wooden buildings burned after mass incendiary attacks on the night of 9 March, a firestorm was created that engulfed much of Tokyo.

Opposite top In the aftermath of the bombing, tens of thousands of charred bodies were found on the streets – men, women and children, the fire burnt them all indiscriminately.

Opposite below A whole section of Tokyo simply disappeared as a result of the fire-bombing, in scenes prescient of the more famous aftermath of the nuclear bombs.

would be tortured, raped or murdered by the Americans if they were captured. It was also made clear to the civilians that it would be shameful to surrender. The role of the army in provoking the tragedy that subsequently occurred is hard to underestimate – as on Saipan, the soldiers knew that they were forbidden to surrender and must have felt desperately concerned for the welfare of any civilians left behind (and perhaps, if one was to view the situation cynically – a little resentful that other Japanese in the vicinity would survive them).

On 27 March around 800 villagers, mostly old men, women and children, gathered in a ravine at the southern end of Tokashiki. The Americans were less than half a mile away. 'The children had been told that they would be killed if the enemy captured them,' says Kinjou, who was there with his mother and brother. 'And also that to be captured would bring great shame – so it was better to choose to die.' Suddenly there was an explosion – a small American bomb had dropped nearby. Then one of the village elders started to kill his family with the branch of a tree. At this sign that a senior member of the group was prepared to sacrifice those whom he loved, other villagers started to follow his example. 'The first person we killed was our own mother,' says Kinjou. 'Our mother who gave us life. Everything around me, including my mind, was in absolute chaos and I don't remember the details. But what I do remember is that we first tried to tie her neck with rope. Finally we took a stone and bashed in her head. That's the brutal thing we did to our mother. I couldn't stop crying because of a sadness that I had never experienced before. I will never cry like that in my life again.' Around 320 men, women and children died in the mass suicide on Tokashiki. After killing their mother, Shigeaki Kinjou and his brother decided to make a suicide charge towards the Americans but were captured alive. 'I think we were dreadfully manipulated,' says Kinjou. 'As I got older my soul started to suffer. It's fifty-five years since the end of the war and I still suffer today.'

Just as with the kamikazes, it is hard for those of us in the West fully to understand the mentality of people like Shigeaki Kinjou and to appreciate why, at the time, committing matricide seemed, incredibly, the proper course of action. What Westerners lack, of course, is the understanding gained by growing up exposed to Japanese cultural values. Even today it is not uncommon in Japan for a disgraced wife to kill her children and then herself. Japan may not have the highest suicide rate in the world, but the suicides that do occur are often of a different kind from those in the West. Suicide is still seen as an 'honourable' way out of an insurmountable problem. The intense desire to remain part of the group is such that in a crisis some people prefer to take their own lives rather than face shame and ostracism. On the island of Tokashiki, what choice did the teenage Shigeaki Kinjou really have on 27 March 1945? Surrounded by his family and members of his community, told that he would be killed (and perhaps tortured first) if he was captured, lectured that the divine emperor himself expected him to die, witness to the village elders killing their own loved ones, what effective alternative was available to him? To run away? But where to? Straight to the 'murderous' Americans? No, like most human beings he chose the path of least resistance – the tragedy was that, in the warped system of values that then prevailed, the course of least resistance was also the path to murder.

It is also important to remember that even those Japanese servicemen committed to the kamikaze cause, like Fujio Hayashi, were never the mindless automatons of Western popular myth. While waiting in vain to be chosen to fly on a mission, Hayashi debated with himself what his last words should be: 'In Japan, when you die you were supposed to say "Banzai!" [Hooray!] to the Emperor. But most of us actually wanted to say "Mother" before we died. But my mother had died when I was small. My father brought me up. But it's hard to say "Father" before dying, in a way. And there was this geisha that I loved very much – her name was Misako – and I thought I would probably scream her name when I crashed into an enemy ship.'

There is a final irony to the kamikaze story – one which reminds us not to believe that all Japanese at the time chose death rather than shame. Warrant Officer Shoichi Ota, the man responsible for the catastrophic 'human missile', was thought to have flown off into the Pacific, never to return, at the end of the war. But naval design technician Tadanao Miki remembers his fate differently: 'I heard the rumour that

Ota had flown his own suicide mission. But I also heard that some years after the war one of my subordinates had bumped into him. It was raining and he lent Ota an umbrella which Ota never returned. Obviously that meant Ota was still alive. But afterwards I don't know what happened to him. Nobody knows what happened to him – it's a mystery.'

But it was a mystery that was solved by the *Timewatch* team during the making of their BBC film on the kamikazes. They discovered that after the war Shoichi Ota had changed his name to Michio Yokoyama and begun a new life. Only in 1994, as he lay seriously ill, did he tell his family about his past. 'We were told he had three months to live,' says his son. 'And it was then that my father revealed things to us which he hadn't told us about before. I had never seen him cry until he said it was his fault that so many young people had died before reaching their twentieth birthday. I couldn't think of anything to say – only that many terrible things happen in war and that no one can be blamed for them.' The tale of Shoichi Ota and his incompetent suicide missile is an important reminder that, even in a culture where the vast majority feel compelled to conform, there were still individuals who preferred to risk shame and ostracism to save themselves.

On Okinawa in the spring of 1945 the US marines engaged in a bitter fight with the determined soldiers of the Imperial Army formed a more simplistic view of their Japanese opponents: 'They were an inhuman race,' says former marine sergeant James Eagleton. 'We had no concern about killing the Japanese. [If] we'd have gone to Japan we'd have probably killed a thousand to one [i.e., 1000 Japanese for every American], but we would have killed 'em without regret.' The 'inhuman race' who were defending the island, under the command of Lieutenant General Mitsuru Ushijima, had adopted a strikingly original tactic. On Okinawa, unlike at Iwo Jima and Saipan, the Imperial Army did not oppose the landing of American troops on the beaches. Instead, the 77,000 Japanese and 20,000 Okinawan support troops had retreated inland to well-prepared defensive structures, often concrete pill-boxes dug into the mountainside. By using this tactic the Japanese sought to demonstrate to the Americans that they could only capture Okinawa at prohibitive cost. Soldiers of the Imperial Army, like Hajime Kondo, simply sat secure in their defences and waited. 'I saw Americans for the first time in my life,' says Kondo. 'Their tanks came first and then the infantry companies followed. The soldiers were carrying guns and they were chewing gum. They looked as though they came for a picnic.' But once the Americans advanced towards the northern mountainous part of the island, the Japanese confronted them. 'We realized that we were losing a lot of people,' says James Eagleton. 'They were very excellent trained troops and killed any number of our company people. You'd get up there and you'd get under machine gun fire and you'd lose people.'

The jungle around the mountains of central Okinawa made it virtually impossible to dislodge the Japanese defenders except by brutal, near hand-to-hand, personal combat. As a result there was a high rate of battle fatigue amongst the marines and, as Eagleton admits, they were 'mentally breaking up' under the strain. One of the most hazardous of duties was to be selected as a night picket. Seven or eight marines would be ordered to set up a defensive line 200 yards or so from where the main unit was resting. The idea was simple – if the Japanese attacked under cover of darkness they would encounter this small force first and the alarm would be raised. The soldiers on picket duty knew all too well that they were unlikely to survive such an attack themselves. And sometimes even when the Japanese did not mount a night action the marines broke down. 'Once they sent out eight marines to set up one of these defences,' says Eagleton. 'That night there wasn't any firing. When they came back, seven of them had battle fatigue. They were crying and were unable to function as marines for a day or two. The one that didn't have battle fatigue, he was a dairy man from New York and I always thought he was too dumb to know what they were out there for.'

Many marines, even though technically not victims of battle fatigue still found that in these conditions, as Eagleton puts it, their 'mental faculties' became abnormal. 'You would see things that didn't exist,' he says. 'One time I saw Japanese attacking our position and all night we fought. Next morning there weren't any Japanese. Mentally I saw the Japanese. I never had that experience before or since.'

The Japanese fought stubbornly on, through April and May. And as Hajime Kondo watched the Americans in their death throes, he made a surprising discovery: 'The Japanese soldier's last word was usually "Mother" – I saw several people die in the war, but nobody called out "Banzai!" for the Emperor. Americans also muttered "Mother" when they died. When we shot them, we heard them calling "Mom" or "Mother". We talked about it amongst ourselves – that when they were dying they said the same thing as us.'

Similar emotions of fellow feeling were distinctly lacking amongst James Eagleton and his comrades. He frankly confessed to us that 'we did not ever take a Japanese prisoner. In the two years that I was overseas I saw no prisoner ever taken. Once thirty or forty of them came out with their hands up. They were killed on the spot because we didn't take prisoners.' Eagleton seeks to justify his actions by saying that 'on Guadalcanal a number of Japanese would come up purporting to surrender, and fall down with grenades under their arms and blow people up. Any number of tricks the Japanese had. We'd call them "Tricky Nipper". We had a Lieutenant James and he was always talking about "Tricky Nipper" and "Don't let that little rascal get close to you."'

'When you yourself were shooting these prisoners who were trying to surrender,' we asked him, 'what was in your mind?'

'We were just defending ourselves.'

'But they had their hands up....'

'That's right.'

James Eagleton admitted that he and his comrades were never given a specific order by his superiors not to take prisoners, but maintains that it was tacitly understood that this was what was required of them. He cites one example that typifies the culture of the time: 'Two fellows running a telephone line across country came across a Japanese who surrendered to them. They took him to the company headquarters and the captain just blew his top. "You've ruined our record!" he said. "Sergeant, take this prisoner to battalion headquarters and I will see you at eleven-fifteen." Well, it was eleven o'clock and the headquarters was 5 miles away. They took him out and killed him.'

The significance of this story is considerable. What it demonstrates, of course, is the inadequacy of Eagleton's explanation as to why he and his comrades shot Japanese troops who tried to surrender to them. The soldier who was shot after his capture had been announced to the company commander and presented no danger. He was killed out of principle, not pragmatism. Neither does it appear to have been essential as a matter of course to shoot Japanese prisoners who attempted to surrender. Archive film exists that shows how many American units dealt with any potential danger from surrendering Japanese. The soldiers were simply ordered, still at some distance from the Americans, to take off their clothes. The Japanese complied, showing that they possessed no concealed weapons and were therefore no threat. Therefore it is hard to escape the conclusion that James Eagleton and his comrades needed little other justification to kill surrendering Japanese soldiers than their hatred of the enemy, and the self-confessed belief that they were fighting 'an inhuman race'.

Of course, any Japanese soldiers who surrendered were themselves breaking their word to their supreme commander, Emperor Hirohito, who had called for them to fight to the death. But on Okinawa thousands did decide to give up, and their surrender was accepted by the Americans. After years of brutal fighting there were signs that significant numbers of Japanese had simply had enough and decided they wanted to survive the war. But Hajime Kondo was not one of them — even after enduring weeks of fighting, suffering a bullet wound to his back and made distraught with lack of sleep and food. 'There was never any thought of surrender,' he says. 'To become a POW is to defame the family.' So after almost all his comrades had been killed — many, he says, 'dying like dogs' in the caves of Okinawa as the Americans burnt them out with flame throwers — he decided in June 1945 that the moment had come for him to meet his own end. 'I thought, it's time to join my colleagues. That's why we decided to attempt a banzai attack. It was suicidal behaviour, but I believed that death would be a kind of relief for us at the time.' He ran towards the Americans with one of his comrades alongside him, but suddenly his friend was shot and, as

Kondo reached down to help him, he stumbled and fell himself. 'I was surrounded by American soldiers. They were pointing guns at me.' He expected them to kill him, but instead, as he gestured that he was thirsty, they offered him water from a canteen. 'Then,' he says, 'I realized that American soldiers are kind.'

Despite the large numbers of Japanese soldiers who did surrender, the majority still decided to fight to the death; and as the Americans pushed the Imperial Army to the south of Okinawa there were many civilian suicides, including several thousand at Cape Kiyan. Once again, the Japanese army played a crucial role in encouraging civilians to kill themselves. Significantly, on nearby islands where there were no Japanese soldiers, there were no mass suicides.

By 22 June 1945 all of Okinawa was finally in American hands. Eight thousand American troops had died on the island, a figure dwarfed by the 60,000 Japanese soldiers and 150,000 Okinawan civilians who had lost their lives in the struggle. And the way some of the American troops behaved towards the civilians who remained on the island will come as a surprise to those in the West who believe that this was a war in which atrocities against civilians were only committed by one side. Teru Yasumura was a young mother of twenty-five when the Americans landed on Okinawa. She was told – in the familiar propaganda way of the Japanese – that the Americans were a 'mad' army and that if they caught Okinawan women they would 'cut their throats'. She confesses that, if her village had been surrounded by the Americans and there had been fighting to capture it, she too would probably have committed suicide. As it was, the Americans simply arrived the day after the Japanese had retreated. But in their wake came further rumours that the occupying forces would do 'all sorts of things' to any women they caught. As a result, Teru and her friends used to try to make themselves 'look unattractive' by rubbing dirt into their faces and tearing their kimonos.

One day, Teru and several other young women from her village were out tending their vegetable plots in a remote area near the mountains of central Okinawa when some American soldiers appeared. The women ran, but one of them was caught by the Americans. Several hours later she reappeared in the village looking dishevelled. Nine months later she gave birth to a baby boy. 'We felt revolted,' says Teru, 'that the Americans could do that to a young girl.' Significantly, little was ever said openly in the village about what happened – even after the young girl who had been raped had given birth. To be raped was a cause for 'shame', and as a result the crime was never reported. The young victim had to endure the silent censure of the other villagers for the rest of her life, and not surprisingly she never married. Because few of the Okinawan women who were raped wish to speak of their experience, it is almost impossible to discover just how common was the crime. But local historians working on Okinawa believe that there were many similar cases in the wake of the American victory.

When interviewed, James Eagleton admitted that in his time in Pacific he 'heard of one man in my group that raped an old woman and was reported to me. I was sergeant of the platoon at the time and I had the problem about what to do about it. Was I to report him to the lieutenant or the company commander? I needed to report him to somebody. But the Japanese took care of it. They killed him with a 91-millimetre mortar shell – landed right on top of him.'

As the Americans celebrated their victory on Okinawa it was obvious to Hirohito and the Japanese leadership that the war was effectively lost – but there was still no agreement on how Japan could end the conflict that was destroying the country. 'The reason why Japan continued the war,' says Masatake Okumiya, then a senior officer in the Imperial Navy, 'is that for the previous half-century, through the first Sino–Japanese War, the Russo–Japanese War, up to World War I, the Japanese had never lost a war. Japan had always won. Thus, both the government and the military people didn't know how to deal with losing a war. They didn't have any experience of defeat and they didn't know how to end it. In that situation, it was easier to continue the war rather than to make the courageous decision to lose it.'

The new prime minister, Kantaro Suzuki, had made attempts in May 1945 to open a line of communication with the Soviet Union in the hope that the Russians could intercede on Japan's behalf with the other Allies.

But the negotiated peace envisioned by the Japanese at this stage was a long way from the unconditional surrender demanded by the Allies. The Japanese military were insisting not just on the Allies agreeing to keep the emperor system intact, but also on their accepting other surrender conditions – such as not occupying the home islands of Japan and giving the Japanese the right to try their own war criminals. This was a package of demands that the Allies would never have accepted.

By June it was clear that two different strategies to end the war were emerging within the Japanese elite. On the one hand there was the attempt to get the Soviet Union to help negotiate a peace, and on the other there was the desire of hard-liners within the army to wait until the Americans landed on the Japanese home islands and presented the Imperial Army with one final opportunity to defeat them.

In July the Allied leaders met at Potsdam in Germany to consider the terms under which Japan's surrender would be accepted. Present at that conference was Harry Truman, who had become President of the USA after Roosevelt's death in April. At Potsdam, he was given news that would radically shape the way the war ended, and would dictate the political strategy of the great powers for many decades. He learnt of the successful test (code-named 'Trinity') of the atomic bomb in the New Mexican desert. 'When word reached the President that the Trinity test was successful,' says George Elsey, then naval aide to the President, 'he was elated – he was very, very pleased. He was delighted… "delighted" is the wrong word… he felt that here was a chance to bring the war to a speedy conclusion, and avoid the loss of American lives.'[2] At Potsdam, Stalin mentioned that he had been asked to intervene on behalf of the Japanese to negotiate a peace, only to be told by the Americans that his help was not required in brokering a settlement with Japan.

In recent years there has been considerable controversy both over the Allied decision not to open peace negotiations at the time of the Potsdam conference and, especially, over the decision to use the atomic bombs a few weeks later. It is true that President Truman did receive advice, from people as disparate as former President Hoover and under-secretary of state Joseph Grew, that unless the Allies agreed to preserve the institution of the emperor there would be no Japanese surrender. Equally, US secretary of state Byrnes did tell Truman that one consequence of using the atomic bomb would be to demonstrate to the Soviet Union the power that the United States now possessed. But none of that means that the prime motivation of the US leadership in deciding to drop the atomic bomb was anything other than the desire to ensure that there was no negotiated settlement with Japan.

Even if the Allies had decided to enter into peace negotiations with Japan at this stage (an act that would have broken the pledge they had previously made about insisting on 'unconditional surrender') it is doubtful whether sufficient consensus existed amongst the Japanese leadership to allow a settlement to be reached. There would have been those in the Japanese elite who would have interpreted the Allies' willingness to negotiate as a sign of weakness. Was this not an indication, they would have argued, of how the Americans had finally become unable to endure the level of human loss that was being inflicted upon them by the heroic defenders of the Imperial Army? Similarly, another obstacle to peace existed in the human form of General Korechika Anami, the army chief of staff, who still intransigently maintained that peace should only be negotiated after the elusive 'decisive victory' had been won on Japanese soil. Thus huge numbers of Japanese troops were digging themselves in on the beaches of Kyushu (the place on the home islands where the Japanese expected the Americans to land) prepared to fight to the death to defend their homeland.

That July, as they pondered what course to take, the American leadership knew, thanks to intelligence intercepts, both about the Japanese attempts to instigate a negotiated peace through the Soviet Union and about the military activity on Kyushu. It is hard to see, from the perspective of the American decision-makers at the time, how the combination of these two events suggested that the Japanese were now anxious to surrender. On the contrary, did not the actions of the Japanese demonstrate that they might merely want a ceasefire in order to string out surrender negotiations while they regrouped? At the front of the American consciousness was the way in which the Japanese had behaved during the discussions immediately preceding the outbreak of war – their delegation had still been negotiating in Washington only days before the US fleet was bombed at Pearl Harbor. Understandably, the Americans were not inclined to take the Japanese government's stated intentions at face value.

For all these reasons Truman decided, just days after the issue of the Potsdam Declaration calling once more for the 'unconditional surrender' of Japan, to order the use of the atomic bomb. A special committee reviewed possible targets and finally recommended that the attack be made on a city on the southwestern end of the main Japanese home island of Honshu – Hiroshima. On 6 August 1945 the American atomic strike force appeared high above the target. 'We could see the bridge,' says Charles Sweeney, pilot of one of the planes that accompanied the B-29 (named the 'Enola Gay') which carried the bomb, 'the bridge in Hiroshima, which was the aiming point which we'd studied. I saw the bomb falling free from his airplane. It was much easier for me to see it than it was for anybody in his airplane to see it. And I thought to myself, "for better or for worse... it's too late now."'

For the citizens of Hiroshima it rapidly became clear that this was no ordinary bombing raid. 'Large drops of rain started to fall heavily on us,' says Suzuko Numata. 'Of course, we didn't know then that the rain was contaminated with radiation. And the rain was black. We got very wet. My leg was soaked through with the black rain. It was at that moment that I suddenly realized that my foot from the ankle down had disappeared.'

'As we tried to run away I saw many victims,' says Akihoro Takahashi, 'their arms held out in front of them and their skin all peeled off, their clothes all in tatters. We were all more or less naked and we were all barefoot. We dragged ourselves along, trying to escape wherever we could. We were just like ghosts, like marching ghosts. I saw a man whose upper body was stuck all over with pieces of glass. There was another man whose upper body had lost all its skin and all we could see was the red, raw flesh. There was a woman whose one eyeball had popped out. I don't remember whether it was the left or the right eye and she was covered in blood. And amongst the corpses I saw a dreadful sight – a woman's body with the intestines burst and scattered all around her on the ground. There was a baby lying next to its dead mother, both with their skin peeled away. The baby was still alive. The baby was crying and crying and crying. I just cannot forget that sound even to this day.'

In a story that demonstrates once again the distancing effect of high altitude bombing, Charles Sweeney reveals that while all of this suffering was taking place on the ground, at 32,000 feet he settled back into his return journey and had lunch: 'I had a sandwich and some pineapple juice – we always had pineapple juice – and then I went back and took a nap. And I woke up and had a cigar, and just kept on boring holes in the sky until we got back to base. After we landed and went through debriefings and made out our reports, there was a big party.'

Events now moved swiftly – all against the Japanese. Forty-eight hours after Hiroshima had been bombed Stalin, anxious to gain influence and territory for the Soviet Union, declared war on Japan and his troops quickly moved against the Imperial Army in Manchuria. The following day, 9 August, having received no communication from the Japanese, the Americans dropped a second atomic bomb on Nagasaki.

The bombing of Hiroshima and Nagaski is seared into the consciousness of the world, and there is still passionate debate about whether it was morally right to use such a terrible weapon. A large part of the controversy rests on the public perception that the atomic bomb was somehow so uniquely horrible that it should never have been used. But that is a position that would surely have been incomprehensible to the hundreds of thousands of Japanese victims of the fire-bombing campaign that preceded the nuclear attacks. Throughout June and July, American bombers conducted incendiary raids on Japanese towns and cities. Indeed, contrary to popular belief, the atomic bomb dropped on Nagasaki was not the last American bomb to fall on Japan. On 14 August Kumagaya was bombed by 'conventional' means – and, significantly, a greater proportion of Kumagaya (45 per cent) was destroyed as a result of this 'conventional' bombing attack than in the atomic raid on Nagasaki (40 per cent destroyed).[3] Yet who in the West has ever heard of the horrific bombing of Kumagaya? Why are the women and children incinerated by nuclear means at Hiroshima and Nagasaki worthy of remembrance in history when the women and children incinerated by fire-bombing in countless other Japanese cities like Kumagaya are not? The truth is that in the context of the American saturation bombing offensive of spring and summer 1945 the nuclear bombs were merely a more effective way of delivering the same result – the elimination of Japanese civilians and the infrastructure of the country. Their use was wholly in character with the bombing policy that preceded them.

In Tokyo, the dropping of the first atomic bomb did nothing to change the mind of die-hards like General Anami. He and several other senior military figures still said that peace must be negotiated and that foreign troops should not be allowed to occupy Japan. But prime minister Suzuki disagreed: he thought the time had come to accept the terms of the Potsdam Declaration. By 10 August – after the bombing of Nagasaki – Hirohito had finally taken the decision that the war must come to an end. A combination of the Soviet advance in Manchuria and fear of more nuclear attacks had finally convinced him to stop vacillating.

Once the Japanese had stated their willingness to accept the terms of the Potsdam Decalaration, the Allies hinted that the institution of the emperor might be kept. This was not 'negotiation' but a pragmatic sign that the Americans, from their position of strength, felt that keeping the Japanese monarchy might make the forthcoming occupation easier. Notwithstanding this shift in the Allied position, on 13 August the Japanese cabinet was divided – still the military hawks could not face the prospect of defeat. On the 14th, in an attempt to break the deadlock, American planes dropped leaflets on Japanese towns and cities announcing that the government had accepted the surrender terms of the Potsdam Declaration. That same day Hirohito reiterated to those around him his determination to end the war on the American terms, but Field Marshals of the Imperial Army told him that the war should carry on. Earlier that day Field Marshal Shunroku Hata, who had just flown up from Hiroshima, had remarked that in his view the atomic bomb was 'not that powerful a weapon'.[4] Hirohito for once stood firm and shortly afterwards recorded a radio speech in which he announced the Japanese surrender – a speech due to be broadcast the following day. But there still remained those in the military who would not accept the will of their supreme commander. On the evening of the 14th fanatical military officers broke into the household ministry, searching for the recording of the emperor's speech and killing the commander of the guard. But the plotters searched in vain and, not receiving support from other military units, committed suicide. On 15 August 1945, Emperor Hirohito's speech announcing the surrender was played to the Japanese people. The war was finally over. General Anami, who had not supported the mutineers, was one of many senior military figures who committed suicide shortly afterwards.

It is significant – indeed, with hindsight astonishing – that there was still a dispute within the Japanese elite about whether Japan should surrender even after the swift gains secured by the Red Army in Manchuria and the dropping of two American atomic bombs. Given such intransigence it is difficult to see how, without the dropping of the atomic bombs, Japan would ever have surrendered without the continuation – and possible escalation – of the fire-bombing campaign.

Whether an invasion of Japan would ever have been subsequently necessary is still one of the great unanswered questions of history. Perhaps a combination of the continued conventional bombing and the threat from the Soviet Union (assuming the Russians would have declared war on Japan even if the first nuclear bomb had not been dropped on Hiroshima) would have forced the Japanese to concede defeat. What is certain is that the statement that dropping the nuclear bombs 'saved Allied lives' is correct, since without the bombs being dropped the Imperial Army would have continued fighting for weeks, perhaps months, in Burma, Borneo, Malaya and elsewhere.

General Douglas McArthur arrived in Yokohama on 31 August to oversee the occupation of Japan. Like most of the American occupying force he was immediately struck by how cooperative the Japanese had suddenly become. Loyalty, obedience, dependability – all the qualities that Japanese citizens had directed towards the military regime –were now turned towards the occupiers. McArthur appeared to the Japanese to be precisely the sort of strong, decisive military figure they were familiar with from their own history – especially as he chose, just like the Shogun, to work behind the figure of the emperor.

Hirohito remained on the throne, though under the American occupation he was a god no more, but a constitutional monarch at the head of a democratic government. And without a doubt the Allied decision to retain Hirohito on the throne did ease the transition of Japan into a democratic state. But there is compelling evidence that the short-term measure of allowing Hirohito to stay as emperor did profound damage to the country's development. Even today Japan is criticized as a nation because of an inability to apologize properly for the crimes committed in the nation's name during the war – and the chief block to that sincere apology is the inability of the Japanese to express criticism for the past without, as a consequence, doing the unthinkable and criticizing the actions of Emperor Hirohito. Japanese society during the war and in the immediate pre-war years was profoundly hierarchical. Each person related to the hierarchy in a way that was much more rigid than even the German or Soviet totalitarian systems. And as they sought instruction from those above them, there was only one individual in the entire structure who was perceived to have 'free will' – the emperor. Of course, his power was constrained by many factors – the information his advisers chose to give him, the traditional role of the emperor as an arbiter rather than a proactive participant, and, not least, the fear that Hirohito must have had of precipitating a coup against him if he crossed the military too much. But none the less, as history shows, Hirohito possessed enormous latent power within the system. A different Japanese emperor – one of stronger character and greater integrity – might have ended the war two years earlier and prevented many of the war crimes that subsequently tarnished the reputation of Japan. The fact that Hirohito not only escaped punishment for his participation in this war of aggression and destruction, but appeared to take no responsibility whatsoever for any of his actions, made it hard for anyone else in Japan to acknowledge truthfully what they themselves had done during the conflict.

In a flawed and in many ways unjust series of trials held by the Allies at the end of the war, around 5000 Japanese were tried for war crimes. But this only served to highlight the immunity of the emperor and grow the fiction that he had been a puppet head of state unable to prevent the horrors that had occurred – a fiction that carefully overlooked the truth that it had been this puppet who, by finally acting decisively, had brought the war to an end. Even if Hirohito had not stood trial, he could have abdicated in favour of the young crown prince, thus preserving the institution of the emperor but still acknowledging his own responsibility. But it was not to be. The supreme commander of the Japanese armed forces, the man in whose name more than a million Japanese soldiers died, stayed on as emperor. 'Why did the person at the top,' asks Hajime Kondo, that rarest of veterans in Japan – a man prepared to speak out about the past, 'why did the person who had supreme responsibility, not take responsibility for the war? I would have expected if the emperor had given any thought to those who died in misery on the front line, he would have taken some responsibility.'

Emperor Hirohito remained on the throne until his death in 1989. As a result, the majority of Japanese people had to learn to develop amnesia about events before 15 August 1945. 'Veterans don't really talk about the war openly,' says Kondo. "Don't talk about bad things," they say, "as it would shame Japan. Keep quiet."'

POSTSCRIPT

Seven years ago I began a journey that was at once physical, intellectual and emotional. Physical because it would take me around the world – from the bourgeois villas of Munich to the high-rise apartments of Tokyo, from the wastes of Siberia to the jungles of Borneo; intellectual because I would have the privilege of seeking answers to my questions from some of the cleverest academics in the world; and emotional because I sought to confront the perpetrators[1] of some of the worst crimes in recent history. Now it is over, and what I discovered was not what I had expected.

Since 1994 I have written and produced a trilogy of projects – each a TV series and a book – on Nazism (*The Nazis: A Warning from History*), on the war between Hitler and Stalin (*War of the Century*) and, finally, on the Japanese experience of the Second World War (*Horror in the East*). Of course, neither I, nor the production teams who worked with me, thought that as subject matter this was virgin territory for television – the military history of the war, for example, had long ago been covered in Jeremy Isaacs' brilliant *The World at War*. But what we did believe was new was our desire to explore the mentality of those who had taken part in the conflict – particularly the mentalities of the perpetrators, those who had committed the murders, the rapes, the war crimes. We had a desire not to excuse their actions, but to try to understand them, to obtain answers to questions that were childlike in their simplicity – how, and why, could they have done such things?

Over the last seven years many people have contributed to the work, but no one person, apart from myself, has worked as a journalist across all three projects. It seemed, so the joke in the office went, as if my appetite for learning about horror was limitless. What was driving me on, however, was not the desire merely to collect different brutal stories from continent to continent, but an increasing feeling as the years passed that, broadly speaking, I was hearing the same stories again and again – only the faces and the countries changed. I felt less and less the importance of national or cultural differences, more and more a common thread that linked all of those who had committed terrible crimes during the war. This kind of comparative historical experience is normally one denied to professional historians, since they are both wary of moving outside of their disciplines – an expert on the Third Reich does not travel to Japan to study Hirohito – and more inclined to study documents than track down and interview the perpetrators in person. So I began to feel that my experience of encountering war criminals across several continents was not only disturbing, it was unique.

When I started my research I had no predetermined theory that I was trying to prove, but I did think that the perpetrators I would meet would be somehow obviously 'evil' in themselves – not that they would have horns exactly, but that they would be demonstrably different from the rest of society. Not a bit of it. The Japanese farmer who raped Chinese women, the Lithuanian peasant who shot Jewish children, the Russian woman who murdered a young German major, all shared one attribute – their apparent normality. In many cases not even their close families had suspected the terrible acts they had committed during the war. Another misconception I had was that they would almost certainly be tortured by guilt as a result of their crimes. Again – not so. The majority of them were not sorry for the crimes they had committed (in fact, most did not think they had committed any crime). Was it correct to kill Jews? 'Well, it was a problem that had to be dealt with.' Was it acceptable to shoot German prisoners after an interrogation? 'Of course, they'd been trying to kill us on the battlefield.' Was it a crime to bayonet Chinese prisoners? 'Well, there was an administrative problem and not all of them could be fed.'

What the majority of the perpetrators I met had in common was this desire to excuse their actions by context. 'If you had been there, you would have done the same,' was their constant refrain. And in their claim that anyone who fully understood the circumstances of their time would recognize that they had not committed any crime at all, these worst of perpetrators were merely repeating the same kind of answers given by most of the people we interviewed who had lived more peacefully through the regimes concerned. There was the nice lady in Munich who told us how she willingly took part in Nazi parades because she and her family thought Hitler was 'doing good' for Germany, the ambitious woman in Kiev who said she had joined the communist party because she thought Stalin 'was a god', and the Japanese gentleman who firmly believed that it was hypocritical of Western countries that had colonies to protest at Japan's expansion into Manchuria. All of these interviewees – many hundreds across Germany, the former Soviet Union and Japan – sought to justify their participation in the regimes concerned by referring only to the immediate circumstances. What made them angry was the paradox that it was the 'law-abiding' people of the time who had become criminals in the eyes of today.

As I travelled from country to country over the years, and thought long and hard about the interviewees' point of view, I began to think there was more than an element of truth in what they were saying. It is not so much that we had been judging the past by today's standards – plenty of people, Winston Churchill amongst them, had warned about the evil of these totalitarian regimes at the time – as that we massively underestimate the willingness of human beings to conform. In Japan, the most conformist of the three societies we examined, the search is always to preserve the harmony of the group. As a result the concept of *geri* is vital. *Geri* is often translated as 'duty', but that is not quite accurate. In the West 'duty' can mean adherence to an abstract idea like 'justice', but in Japan *geri* is defined only by the group. Ethical values are what the leadership say are ethical values – and in the 1930s that meant the emperor was a god and the Chinese were subhuman. Japanese school-children learnt these corrupted values and were told they were honourable. Once that kind of idea is put into your brain as a child it is hard to get it out without living through a revolution. Similarly, under Nazi rule in Germany in the 1930s, the mass of people simply wanted to lead quiet, contented lives – if that meant adapting to the new values of Nazism then so be it. Witness this mournful report written in 1936 by a member of one of the outlawed opposition parties, the SPD:

'The average worker is primarily interested in work and not in democracy. People who previously enthusiastically supported democracy show no interest at all in politics. One must be clear about the fact that in the first instance men are fathers of families and have jobs, and that for them politics take second place and even then only when they expect to get something out of it.'[2]

And before British readers react smugly, thinking there is something inherently Japanese or German or Russian about this desire to conform and not cause trouble, remember the research that has recently been completed about collaboration in the German-occupied Channel Islands during the Second World War – the pleasant climate, the friendly popu- lation (a number of local girls married German soldiers) and the lack of any real threat from a resistance group meant that the Channel Islands were the German military man's dream posting.

This is not to say, I hasten to add, that I believe this longing to con- form to the values of the group is something that is inherently weak. It is not that these Germans or Japanese or Russians for the most part went along with the regimes concerned against their better judgement at the time. No, because of what psychologists call 'the situational ethic', their better judgement *was* that by conforming they were doing the right thing. It is only afterwards that they can sometimes look back in wonder at what they did. The enormous importance of this 'situational ethic' in understanding why people acted as they did came to me with greatest force several years ago as I was sitting in the front room of a small, neat house on the Baltic coast of what had until recently been East Germany. We were interviewing a charming, helpful old man who was telling us how, as a teenage member of the Hitler Youth, he had taken part in the fighting against the advancing Red Army. Only after the interview, as we sat over a cup of tea, did I discover his subsequent career: from being a fanatical member of the Hitler Youth, he had gone on to become a committed communist, rising to become mayor of the town. And now that communism had gone? He was an utterly committed capitalist entrepreneur, with a thriving business.

And this desire to please whoever is in control demonstrably extends across continental boundaries. A few years after meeting this chameleon-like German, I sat in a traditional Japanese inn in Tokyo and listened to a veteran of the Imperial Army explain how he had moved swiftly from being the member of his platoon most keen to bayonet Chinese prisoners, to being the most cooperative war criminal held by the Chinese after the war. 'The Chinese praised me and said I always wrote the longest and most accurate confessions,' he told us without a hint of irony. His move from best murderer to best prisoner was seamless.

It is easy to react cynically to these kinds of story, thinking that each of us is somehow different from these veterans who so swiftly adapted to their changing world. But look at your own life and think how many of the beliefs and values you hold are genuinely inherently 'yours' and how many are products of the situation. For example, when I was at Oxford the vast majority of colleges did not admit women – something that now I think was indefensibly sexist, but I don't remember saying (or even thinking) so at the time. I just went along with the system because it was the way things were. Similarly, when I first visited Hong Kong and saw it ruled by the British I didn't think there was anything abnormal with that state of affairs. Only on a recent visit when a Chinese friend said 'didn't you ever ask yourself what right did you British ever have to be here telling us what to do?' did I think, 'Ah…. Maybe she's got a point.'

In my immediate family, I remember an uncle of mine – a man who was enormously kind and generous – telling me twenty years ago that homosexuals were 'unnatural' and 'bad'; a view that today would rightfully have him condemned as a bigot were he still alive to express it. But it is easy to forget that my uncle was born in 1905 and until his retirement lived in a society that proclaimed homosexuality to be illegal – so it is hardly surprising that my conformist uncle held the view he did. Had he been born at a different time he would almost certainly have held a different view.

But it is still hard for those of us who live in a relatively peaceful, democratic society to recognize that the ethical values around us can appear to shift fundamentally according to the situation. Ask, for example, a respectable young mother if she would ever consider resorting to prostitution and she will – almost certainly – say no. But thousands of respectable mothers turned to prostitution in Germany in the immediate aftermath of the war in order to feed their children. These mothers had not suddenly become less moral – they were simply responding to a change in the situational ethic.

Even on the Allied side the 'ethics' that governed military behaviour during the Second World War were subject to change. As demonstrated earlier in this book, the Allies altered their attitude to the ethical question of bombing enemy cities. At the start of the war it was a crime – by the end it was legitimate. Even the use of poison gas was considered by the British during the war. In an extraordinary memorandum to the military chiefs of staff, written on 6 July 1944, at the height of the threat from the German flying bombs, Winston Churchill stated:

'I want you to think very seriously over the question of using poison gas. I would not use it unless it could be shown that (a) it was life or death for us, or (b) that it would shorten the war by a year. It is absurd to consider morality on this topic when everybody used it in the last war without a word of complaint from the moralists or the Church. On the other hand, in the last war the bombing of open cities was regarded as forbidden. Now everybody does it as a matter of course. It is simply a question of fashion changing as she does between long and short skirts for women.'[3]

Later in the same memo Churchill says: 'I do not see why we should always have all the disadvantages of being the gentleman while they [i.e., the Germans] have all the advantages of being the cad.' Even though, in the end, Churchill decided that poison gas should not be used, the memo demonstrates conclusively that even one of the most moral and steadfast politicians in British history clearly recognized the reality of the situational ethic.

Part of my initial problem in grasping the central truth of the situational ethic when applied to the perpetrators I encountered was to do with terminology. I persisted in calling them 'war criminals'. And indeed they had committed the most awful crimes. Yet in conventional terms a 'criminal' is someone who operates outside the law – by definition a non-conformist. But the perpetrators I met who had committed the most appalling crimes were precisely the ones who were most keen to work within the law at the time. They were normally ambitious, hardworking, conformist, committed individuals, like the Soviet military intelligence officer who, because military bosses said it was 'right' to do so, tortured prisoners during interrogation and then shot them, or the Japanese and German soldiers who accepted the rhetoric that their (Chinese and Russians) enemies were 'subhuman' and so murdered innocent women and children.

Heinrich Müller, the notorious head of the Gestapo in Nazi Germany, was clearly another of these creatures of the situational ethic. An appraisal by his local Nazi party headquarters in 1937 questioned his deep-rooted commitment to Nazism, saying:

'It must be acknowledged that he proceeded against these [leftwing] movements with great severity.... It is not less clear, however, that Müller, had it been his task, would have proceeded just the same against the right.... With his vast ambition and relentless drive, he would have done everything to gain the appreciation of whoever might happen to be his boss in a given system.'[4]

So even the local Nazis recognized Müller's pragmatic approach to his work as a secret policeman. As long as the Nazis were in control, he would serve them to the best of his ability, but if the communists ever came to power, he would change sides and do his best to persecute the

Nazis. (Fascinatingly, this negative appraisal by his local Nazi party was no bar to Müller's advancement – clearly Himmler, Müller's boss, also understood the truth of the situational ethic. The leader of the SS must have realized that if he were to sack all the opportunistic Nazis he employed, he would not be able to staff the Gestapo.)

What all this led me to was the opposite conclusion to the one I had been expecting to reach – the perpetrators of these terrible acts were not the 'criminal' outcasts I had been expecting to meet, but the ambitious achievers at the centre of their societies who wanted to rise in their careers. It was hardly surprising, therefore, that they seemed 'normal' when one met them.

Of course, it is self-evident that not all war criminals fit into this 'conformist' mode. Two of the greatest war criminals of the twentieth century, Hitler and Stalin, were anything but adherents to the 'situational ethic' of the time; as young men both were terrorists, and both succeeded in destroying the political systems in which they grew up. Neither were the immediate followers of these two dictators creatures of the herd – Himmler took part in the infamous Beer Hall Putsch in 1923, and Molotov was a revolutionary Bolshevik in 1905 at the age of fifteen. Such men were not the followers of the situational ethic but the shapers of it. But, long dead as they were, these were not the kind of war criminals I was encountering on my travels. The vast majority of those I met were the people who had wanted to fit into the new society created by the revolutionaries – and there was a crowd of them. Once it was clear, for example, by March 1933 that Hitler was secure in power, there was a massive surge in applications to join the Nazi party – so much so that these new members were known by the none-too-flattering sobriquet 'March Violets'.

Thankfully, not everyone from the former totalitarian regimes whom I encountered was such a conformist. I did meet a small number of people who had refused to go along with the system, who had believed they were living in an unjust society and who had fought back. But, so the paradox continues, they were the very people who were labelled 'criminal' by society at the time, and even today they often still exude a principled approach to the world that would brand them 'awk-ward'. Indeed, they – not the perpetrators I met – are the ones who are most demonstrably different from the rest of contemporary society. Take the example of the former member of the German communist party I met who returned to Germany once the Nazis were in power, knowing the profound danger he faced, and was then tortured and imprisoned in a concentration camp. He never gave up his belief in communism, even though he knew that if he did he would receive better treatment. Or consider the Russian I encountered who had printed leaflets – knowing the terrible risk he was running – protesting at the arrest of his teacher during one of Stalin's purges. Arrested and imprisoned in a gulag, he vol-unteered to serve in a penal battalion during the war. He cheated the odds and survived – only to be persecuted for the rest of his working life. Listening to his story, I grew more and more bewildered – what was the point, I asked him, of protesting about the arrest of his teacher in the way he did? Surely he must have known it would accomplish nothing but his own imprisonment and misery? As he sat today in his tiny, threadbare Moscow flat, did he not regret what he had done? He paused and then answered: 'I don't regret it at all. At least I have my self-respect.'

But even 'resisters' within corrupt societies can be divided into those truly exceptional human beings who stand out for principle, and those who begin resisting at the moment when it is expedient for them to do so. It is no accident that the bomb plot against Hitler by senior German army officers was not launched until July 1944, when it was clear that the war was lost. It was obviously not in the interests of most officers to kill their Führer in the summer of 1940 when the war was going well for Germany. Equally, as recent research into the French 'resistance' has shown, it was not until it was clear the German army was in trouble that the ranks of the resisters swelled. For much of the war there was very little armed resistance at all.

Thus the final conclusion I reached was that the truly exceptional members of the totalitarian societies I examined were not the war crim-inals who had sought to please their masters, but either the people who resisted the established (and flourishing) oppressive regime or the people who initially created it. These were the people who lived at the edges of society and who were prepared to sacrifice themselves for a cause. But such human beings are rare. The vast majority just wish to go with the flow — and even if that flow happens to be a corrupt and evil one, then they still go along with it. There are very many people, today judged 'criminal' because they tried to live and prosper in that kind of corrupt society, who at the time thought they were normal, law-abiding, boss-pleasing creatures. And the question we should all ask ourselves is whether in the same situation we would be among these people? Maybe one would not have been so careerist as to join the SS (though thousands upon thousands of people wanting to get ahead in Germany did), but how would one have reacted when the Jewish family next door suddenly disappeared? Would one have started to ask questions or simply have looked the other way? Of course, in the end none of us will ever know for sure how we would react until — God forbid — we are forced by circumstance to make the decision. But, statistically, it is clear that only the smallest minority in a successful totalitarian state ever try to resist. As a German who lived through the Third Reich put it to me when I pressed him on why he chose not to fight back against Hitler: 'The trouble with the world today is people who haven't been tested go around making judgements about people who have been tested.'

Thankfully the years since the end of the Second World War have seen an attempt to codify *absolute* standards of human behaviour — something that international law has never effectively done before. Victory over the cruel regimes in Germany and Japan led to such important initiatives as the Universal Declaration of Human Rights and, in more recent years, the European Convention on Human Rights. Such international codification of the proper standards by which human beings should live is the only effective weapon against the vagaries of the situational ethic (though it is significant that it took the international community so very long to agree that torture, slavery, false imprisonment, and discrimination on grounds of race, sex or religion are, under all circumstances, wrong). But the battle is not yet won — demonstrably, the shifting ethic is still with us. It was not until the 1960s that institutional racism began to be tackled in

Britain and the USA – and some say it still exists today. And the situational ethic is alive and flourishing in international affairs. Slobodan Milosovic is charged as a war criminal – but only after he invades Kosovo and the West believes he must be stopped, not when he commits crimes during the war in Bosnia; Saddam Hussein is decreed to be an international war criminal – but only after he invades Kuwait and threatens the West's oil supply, not when he presides over a conflict rich in war crimes against Iran. And in China, what of the people involved in the appalling ethnic cleansing of Tibet? It is unlikely in the extreme that they will ever be brought to the International Court in the Hague to be charged with crimes against humanity. The world needs to get along with China, and the pragmatic reality is that most Western nations care more about their own economic self-interest than the international enforcement of universal standards of human rights.

If there is one lesson to be learnt from all this, then that lesson is also a warning – human beings take considerably more of their ethical values from the particular system they happen to be in at the time than you would ever have thought possible.

Worrying, isn't it?

REFERENCES

THE CHINA SOLUTION

1 See p. 19, Edwin P. Hoyt, *Japan's War*, Da Capo Press, New York, 1986
2 Hoyt, *Japan's War*, p. 95
3 Quoted p. 81, Edward J. Drea, *In the Service of the Emperor*, University of Nebraska Press, 1998
4 Quoted p. 125, Hoyt, *Japan's War*
5 See p. 2, Hoyt, *Japan's War*
6 Quoted p. 38, Iris Chang, *The Rape of Nanking*, Penguin Books, 1998
7 Quoted p. 10, Timothy Brook (ed.), *Documents on the Rape of Nanking*, University of Michigan Press, 2000
8 Quoted pp. 76–7, *The Good Man of Nanking, the diaries of John Rabe*, Vintage Books, 2000
9 Quoted pp. 214–15, Brook (ed.), *Documents on the Rape of Nanking*
10 Quoted p. 99, Yuki Tanaka, *Hidden Horrors, Japanese War Crimes in World War II*, Westview Press, 1998
11 Tanaka, *Hidden Horrors*, p. 99
12 See p. 85, Drea, *In the Service of the Emperor*
13 See p. 343, Herbert P. Bix, *Hirohito and the Making of Modern Japan*, HarperCollins, 2000
14 See p. 206, Edward Behr, *Hirohito, Behind the Myth*, Random House, 1989
15 See p. 59, Sheldon H. Harris, *Factories of Death, Japanese Biological Warfare, 1932–45, and the American Cover-up*, by Sheldon H. Harris, Routledge, 1994

DEALING WITH THE WEST

1 Bix, *Hirohito and the Making of Modern Japan*, p. 249
2 See p. 26, Akira Iriye, *The Origins of the Second World War in Asia and the Pacific*, Longman UK, 1987

3 Iriye, *The Origins of the Second World War in Asia and the Pacific*, p. 34
4 Quoted p. 251, Bix, *Hirohito and the Making of Modern Japan*
5 Reported in *New York Times*, 23 September 1937
6 Quoted p. 154, John W. Dower, *War Without Mercy*, Pantheon Books, New York, 1986
7 Dower, *War Without Mercy*, p. 107
8 Dower, *War Without Mercy*, p. 99
9 See p. 66, Iriye, *The Origins of the Second World War in Asia and the Pacific*
10 Iriye, *The Origins of the Second World War in Asia and the Pacific*, p. 81
11 Quoted p. 195, Hoyt, *Japan's War*
12 Hoyt, *Japan's War*, p. 199
13 See p. 46, Laurence Rees, *War of the Century*, BBC Books, 1999
14 See p. 212, Hoyt, *Japan's War*
15 Hoyt, *Japan's War*
16 Churchill in a letter to Sir Hastings Ismay, chief of the imperial defence staff, in early 1941
17 Quoted p. 101, Dower, *War Without Mercy*
18 See p. 72, John Keegan (ed.), *Times Atlas of WWII* edited by John Keegan
19 Quoted p. 1009, I.C.B Dear and M.R.D Foot (eds.), *The Oxford Companion to the Second World War*, Oxford University Press, 1995
20 Quoted p. 310, Behr, *Hirohito, Behind the Myth*

PRISONERS OF THE JAPANESE

1 See p. 93, Tanaka, *Hidden Horrors*
2 Tanaka, *Hidden Horrors*, p. 12
3 Yoshio Tshuchiya was imprisoned after the war by the Chinese for war crimes
4 Tanaka, *Hidden Horrors*, p. 66. Note

that Murozimi's evidence was
disputed. See *Hidden Horrors,* pp.
11–78, for a full analysis of the war
crimes at Sandakan and Professor
Tanaka's own compelling analysis

5   Statistics quoted p. 2, Tanaka, *Hidden
Horrors*

7   See p. 60, Rees, *War of the Century*

8   Quoted p. 112, Tanaka, *Hidden Horrors*

9   Tanaka, *Hidden Horrors*, p. 121

10 Tanaka, *Hidden Horrors*, p. 129. Order
issued 18 November 1944

LURCHING TOWARDS DEFEAT

1   Quoted p. 432, Bix, *Hirohito and the
Making of Modern Japan*

2   Quoted p. 36, Dower, *War Without
Mercy*

3   Quoted p. 1103, Dear and Foot (eds.),
*The Oxford Companion to the Second World
War*

4   Quoted p. 71, Dower, *War Without
Mercy*

5   Quoted p. 188, Drea, *In the Service of
the Emperor*

6   After the war Michael Witowich had
years of treatment for post-traumatic
stress as a result, in particular, of his
experiences on Saipan

7   The kamikaze interview material in
this chapter (with the exception of the
interview with Kenichiro Oonuki) is
taken from the BBC film *Kamikaze*,
shown in the *Timewatch* series in 1995
and published here for the first time.
The present author is the editor of the
series and the film was written and
produced by Jonathan Stamp

ENDGAME

1   Though note that the most often

quoted number of marines killed in the
battle of Iwo Jima is around 6000

2   This testimony, and the testimony of
Charles Sweeney, Suzuko Numata and
Akihoro Takahashi that follow, come
from interviews contained in *Hiroshima
– the Decision to Drop the Bomb*,
transmitted on BBC1 on 6 August
1995. The executive producer of this
programme for the BBC was the
present author and the film was a
production of Antelope (UK) Ltd,
written and produced by Jeremy
Bennett, executive producer for
Antelope Mick Csáky

3   Figures quoted p. 197, Keegan (ed.),
The Times Atlas of WWII

4   See p. 214, Drea, *In the Service of the
Emperor*

POSTSCRIPT

1   I am aware of the academic debate
about the use of the word 'perpetrator'
and – as much of the current academic
thinking emphasizes – that there were
'perpetrators' during the war who did
subsequently become 'victims'.

2   Quoted p. 591, J. Noakes and
G. Pridham (ed.), *Nazism 1939–1945,
Vol. 2: State, Economy and Society
1933–1939*, University of Exeter
Press, 1984

3   Public Record Office, London, PREM
3/89, quoted pp. 127–9 in Robert
Harris and Jeremy Paxman, *Higher
Form of Killing*, Chatto and Windus,
1982

4   Quoted pp. 55–6, Robert Gellately,
The Gestapo and German Society, Oxford
University Press, 1991

ACKNOWLEDGEMENTS

As this is a book based on a television series there are a large number of people I need to thank. Jane Root, Controller of BBC2, commissioned the series, and without her commitment and subsequent help there would have been no television series and no book. My other bosses, Paul Hamann, then Head of Documentaries and History, and Glenwyn Benson, Controller of Specialist Factual Programmes, were both also extremely supportive. My co-producers at History Channel in America, particularly Charlie Maday and Joe LaPolla, were always a fount of good advice, as was my German co-producer Volker Zielke of NDR in Hamburg.

Professor Akira Iriye of Harvard University was a wonderfully understanding and academically incisive series historical consultant; Professor Yuki Tanaka and Professor Sheldon Harris made a similarly essential contribution to the project. In Japan Professor Tokushi Kasahara, Professor Yutaka Yoshida and Professor Herbert Bix (author of the brilliant recent biography of Hirohito) were especially helpful to us. In Hong Kong we benefited greatly from the work of Jason Wordie, in Borneo Jon Rees and Doris Wong proved of invaluable assistance, in China Hong Qian did a terrific job, in Japan Miho Kometani did fine additional research for us, whilst in Australia Ian Affleck was of sterling aid.

Based in London, Martina Balazova was the Associate Producer on the series – she conducted many of the interviews herself and always proved to be a first-rate journalist on whom I could depend absolutely. Our Japanese Assistant Producer, Fumio Kanda Lai-Hung, also did essential work – much of the original journalism in this project is a direct result of her tenacity and commitment. Tanya Batchelor did a first-rate job as a researcher. Archive research was diligently completed by Jane Mercer, and John Kennedy devised powerful graphics for the series. Alan Lygo edited both programmes with the great artistry we have come to expect. Of the many camera crews who worked with us special mention must be made of Martin Patmore and Brian Biffin, who once again travelled to inhospitable parts of the globe with me and kept their cheerful dispositions intact.

Lorraine Selwyn was a dedicated Production Manager of the project and Nancy Strang, my own assistant, was always generous in her support. Ann Cattini, Unit Manager of the series, and now Production Executive of BBC History Programmes, was also an essential part of the production team, so much so that this book is dedicated to her. For many years now she has not just managed financially all the history productions with which I have been involved, but has also made a vital creative contribution to each one of them. It is important for me to recognize here her vital work on this project (and the previous ones). Any success that these series have had is to a large extent thanks to her.

At BBC Books Sally Potter, Sue Kerr and Nicholas Brett were always kind and helpful, and Andrew Nurnberg also gave sound advice as ever. My dear friend Professor Ian Kershaw kindly read a draft of the Postscript to this book and made a number of useful comments. Professor Iriye not only wrote the generous introduction to this book, he also read the work in manuscript and corrected a number of errors (any that remain are my responsibility).

Of course, I also thank all of the interviewees whose names appear in the body of the book. It is a privilege to be able to question people who have had their kind of extraordinary experiences, and I am grateful to every one of them for agreeing to be interviewed.

Finally, as this is the last of this trilogy of projects, I reserve my closing thanks to my family; to Oliver, Camilla and Benedict, but most of all to Helena. What I owe her can't be put into words.

INDEX